THE IMPROVEMENT
TOOLBOX

THE IMPROVEMENT TOOLBOX

'Every Manager's Guide' to creating long-lasting improvement in your organization

KEITH N. MILES

Streamlined Management Group Inc.
Toronto, Canada

"The Best Management Tool I've Seen In 10 Years!"
Beth Tarter VP Human Resources, OpenText Corporation

Cover / Layout Design: The Riordon Design Group Inc.

For more information, please contact:
Streamlined Management Group Inc.,
P.O. Box 31031
Guelph, Ontario, N1H 8K1
Canada

First Printing 1997
Second Printing 1999
Printed on recycled paper.

ISBN   0-9681291-0-2

Attention: Organizations

Specialized versions of The Improvement Toolbox can be produced for volume situations.

Quantity discounts are available for bulk purchases.

Special excerpts can be created for specific needs.

Contact:

Business Development Manager

Streamlined Management Group Inc.

P.O. Box 31031, Guelph, Ontario N1H 8K1

Phone: (519) 822-3400   Fax: (519) 822-0333

Email: bus.devl@streamlined-group.com

Web: www.streamlined-group.com

This book is dedicated to managers.

To managers who try to make a difference. They balance conflicting interests and still wish to see their organizations and colleagues prosper. May this book provide some of the practical assistance they have been asking for.

Acknowledgements:

The Improvement Toolbox was a team effort. I would like to thank:

The Lord Jesus Christ for wisdom given and guidance in the work. Long before it became fashionable, He was in the recycling business. I continually draw on His recycling services.

My dear wife Nancy for reading, re-reading and putting up with me.

My twin brother Neil for unfailing encouragement.

The initial editors and support team, including Pam Healey, Tony Slegers, Brian Tithecott, Bruce Fournier, and Ken Cook.

Ann Middleton for her terrific editing and proofing.

Ric Riordon and his amazing staff for outstanding design ideas: "How do you choose?"

And finally, our clients and research group members, who teach us as much as we teach them.

CONTENTS

1

Introduction
The Next Stage—Activity Focus

THE IMPROVEMENT TOOLBOX IS ABOUT *CHANGING ACTIVITIES* and how you as a manager, can make simple adjustments to shape employee behavior. The Improvement Toolbox is about constructing jobs that encourage positive behavior rather than asking you to spend time prodding, nagging, and controlling to see changes occur.

The Improvement Toolbox provides you with uncomplicated tools that people will actually use to improve their area's performance.

The Improvement Toolbox quickly shows you two essentials:

1. The steps to ensure that important activities stay important;

2. How to improve the performance of your area.

The Improvement Toolbox teaches you how to create jobs that encourage specific activities. Its simple format for the review of your business situation also provides a guide to help you explain to employees what must be done to make your organization successful. Then you can streamline necessary processes, improve service delivery, and still have time left over to practice your coaching skills. The Improvement Toolbox shows you how.

The Improvement Toolbox is practical, focused and to the point. If your area requires change or improvement, this book will save you and your organization time, money, and frustration.

Warning: If you follow the steps outlined in this book, you will have more time to manage; your area will run more effectively; and you may be promoted to help other areas within your company.

Streamlined Management Group Inc. (SMG) is a management consulting firm that provides managers with effective tools and practical techniques for *changing* activities. The Improvement Toolbox is based on extensive research and field testing, conducted over four years with over 60 organizations.

The Improvement Toolbox describes a method that works. It is easy to understand, realistic, and ready for you to use.

The Core Of The Book

The Improvement Toolbox is based on two fundamentals: the right structure and the right tools.

THE RIGHT STRUCTURE

The majority of employees behave the way they do because their job structures encourage or discourage certain activities. *Performance targets, measures, rewards, incentives, and management attention (or criticism) are examples of job structures.* **Job structures are the elements in a working environment that influence employee behavior.**

Changing activities requires more than talk. It is necessary to change the structures that drive behavior in the company. This means developing structural elements to encourage required activities in the face of the organization's constantly changing priorities. The required activities must be reinforced. Otherwise they fade away when management attention shifts to other issues.

The Improvement Toolbox is about encouraging specific activities and removing obstacles rather than coercing employees. It shows a manager how to fashion a positive context in which the prevailing structures encourage employees to act in the company's best interests.

THE RIGHT TOOLS

Most improvement tools currently being taught are too complex and time-consuming for managers or employees to comfortably use over a period of time. Individuals who normally deal with an issue in 15 minutes will not use a tool that requires hours or days to complete. The Improvement Toolbox describes simple, effective tools that can quickly be used by the majority of employees. It is better to provide uncomplicated techniques that are actually used, rather than teach elaborate ones that are never adopted.

HELP FOR MANAGERS

Why is this important? Aren't existing techniques or programs sufficient? There is growing management frustration with programs that promise real change but do not deliver. Adjusting behavior requires more than a new idea or a catchy phrase. Managers listen to the concepts but are left to sort out the implementation details on their own. Talking about changing perspectives is one thing. Actually helping employees to *behave* differently is much more elusive.

Managers are waiting for help.

Managers need help *doing*. The Improvement Toolbox gives managers a model to follow when activity and behavior changes must be made. Managers need to know how to combine the right structure and the right tools to bring about sustained action.

HELP BASED ON RESEARCH

SMG's research found that successful projects were often accompanied by structure changes in the organizations studied. These modifications encouraged the behavior required for the project's success. For example, changes to existing performance measures or employee evaluation criteria were enough to sustain needed activities in some situations. The Improvement Toolbox is based on this research. Once managers grasp the principles in The Improvement Toolbox, activity changes are possible.

The following model describes the transition through which most organizations are attempting to navigate.

Stage 1 To Stage 2

Organizations have tried a number of programs to improve performance. There have been many success stories and significant achievements. The goals of improvement programs are worth pursuing, but success requires genuine changes in daily activities and routines.

Stage 1 programs, however, are better at changing perspectives than changing activities. They promote the need for change without providing the tools, understanding, or outline needed to bring about activity changes.

A few organizations have made the transition to Stage 2. They have made actual changes to activities. The Improvement Toolbox contains a pattern you can follow. It is a guide book for moving to the activity focus of Stage 2.

Stage 1 Focus: Perspectives

After pursuing popular improvement programs, many organizations have certain points in common. We classify these organizations as Stage 1:

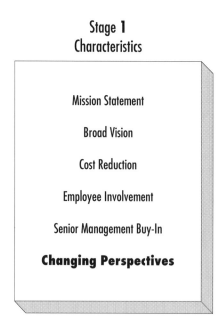

Stage 1
Characteristics

Mission Statement

Broad Vision

Cost Reduction

Employee Involvement

Senior Management Buy-In

Changing Perspectives

Stage 1 companies have developed a mission statement to summarize core values and the organization's purpose. They have expanded the mission statement into a broad or general vision of where the organization is headed. They have finished one or two rounds of cost reductions. The objective was to reduce costs by picking the low fruit or finding easy opportunities to correct product or service problems. Some of the more enthusiastic (or frightened) employees were involved in the cost reduction efforts and perhaps in the development of the mission or vision statement. However, many employees are reluctant to become involved in other changes due to the memory of past company practices, poor role models, or both. Senior management has adopted the jargon and is committed to continuing to reduce costs and involve employees. But further down the organizational chart, cynicism is more common than enthusiasm. The employees and line managers are waiting for concrete signs of commitment rather than more speeches.

Stage 1 programs are effective at convincing employees to consider new ideas. A mission statement created by all the employees and managers can be a way to communicate what is important in the organization. If management action corresponds with those ideals, it can be a positive experience. If prevailing practices do not line up with the mission statement, employee cynicism increases.

Many Stage 1 companies stop progressing after a promising start. *Fatigue* sets in. Employees and managers lose patience with waves of new ideas. They are not interested in learning more *thinking* material. Managers want help *doing* things differently. After Stage 1, managers understand that changes are required, but are not clear how to actually go about changing activities.

Stage 2 Focus: Activities

Doing is Stage 2's strong suit. Stage 2 organizations have a number of things in common:

Stage 2
Characteristics

Strategy - Activity Link

3-Dimensional (Faceted) Vision

Process Management

Employees Engaged

Line Management Buy-In

Changing Activities

They have moved past, but not away from the mission statement. The intent is to change *activities* so that they align with both the mission and strategy. Linking activities with strategy involves looking for the practical requirements and ensuring *activities* match strategic requirements. Rather than be content with a broad vision, they now understand the need to communicate the *activities* that will enable the organization to continue to perform well. Their cost reduction efforts have given way to a focus on managing core processes. Employees are engaged (or responsible) and accountable for the day-to-day management and ongoing improvement of these processes. Whereas in Stage 1, senior management was convinced of the merits of change, now line management is involved and accountable for specific activities. For all levels, Stage 2 organizations have constructed jobs that advance specific activities.

The transition from Stage 1 to Stage 2 involves moving from changing employee perspectives to changing practices and encouraging definite activities.

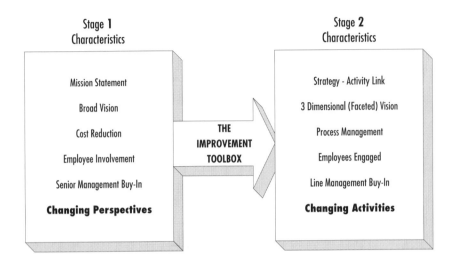

The improvement method presented in The Improvement Toolbox does not replace Stage 1 programs, which are effective in helping people to recognize new possibilities. It is Stage 2 organizations, however, that deliver on the promises made during Stage 1.

There is very little practical help available to equip managers for the activity focus of Stage 2. One executive complained that some organizations make Stage 2 promises, then deliver Stage 1 material without any implementation support. That is why The Improvement Toolbox was written.

The Improvement Toolbox is a manual for Stage 2 organizations. It provides the essential tools needed for successful transition to Stage 2. The Improvement Toolbox gives managers the skills to do the job.

Specific Improvement Programs

There are a number of improvement programs that deserve mention. Though their focus is different, they involve similar goals. Each is beneficial in certain situations, but misses a critical element. These programs need to combine the right structure and the right tools to encourage changed activities.

Because of their lack of an activity orientation, we classify them as Stage 1 programs. The following programs are reviewed: reengineering, teams, technology, quality standards, and principle-based individual change.

REENGINEERING

Reengineering targets rapid, major organizational change. The program focuses on customer needs, quickly fabricates new operating methods, and abandons current practices (if necessary).

Reengineering assumes that an organization has moved so far from its necessary activities that the only option is radical surgery. However, many organizations discover that the pre-reengineering collection of activities was not altogether wrong. The reengineering effort goes full circle, arriving back at the original set of activities with some supposedly essential modifications. The team suggests changes but often leaves many of the previous reinforcing mechanisms in place, perpetuating the same activities with the same problems.

Holding this massive change together requires substantial organizational power. While extreme measures are appropriate to organizations on the brink of failure, this approach can lead to less than positive results for other companies.

The resulting new organization looks surprisingly like the old one. The deadline limits the time available to listen to employee concerns, so employees feel used and are less willing to trust management in the future. One senior bank executive discussed the impact of his company's several-million-dollar reinvention. He said, "It's like nothing changed except a few titles. We're exactly like we were before."

Most organizations don't need radical surgery. They need to review processes and structures to make sure required behavior continues. This method is simpler, less risky, less expensive, and meets the original objectives.

TEAMS

Some organizations spend heavily on retreats, mountain climbing expeditions, and personality assessments. The objective is to form a team with the right makeup of personalities, a healthy sense of trust, and effective communication skills. The assumption is that with an adequate team leading the way, the organization should be able to accomplish necessary changes.

A management team with these characteristics would be enviable, but this approach leaves untouched the job structures that shape employee behavior.

TECHNOLOGY

"If we just had a better computer system, we could increase performance and individual employee effectiveness." Information accessibility is a key success factor for organizations seeking to improve performance. Organizations need systems designed to fit their unique needs. There are many powerful examples of technology-assisted improvements. There are also many examples of implementations that didn't live up to expectations.

Systems often entrench current, pre-improvement steps and activities in programming. This makes ongoing improvement difficult. They frequently add complexity without changing the mechanisms that drive employee behavior. One system being implemented in many large corporations requires the configuration of several thousand interacting tables to determine how the system functions. Many corporations struggle with that level of complexity.

Technology *can* facilitate improvement but processes should be improved and job structures reviewed *before* creating specifications for a new system. In this way, the new system can help to reinforce effective behavior.

QUALITY STANDARDS

Many organizations believe that documenting existing processes to achieve an audited quality standard will improve performance. Reviewing current practices can uncover errors and needless steps. Some companies use the standards as a reason to make needed changes, but many move as quickly as possible through the hoops due to marketing pressures.

If employees don't personally see performance changes during the documentation process, the quality standards are seen for what they often are—marketing support. In addition, the amount of documentation that must be changed and coordinated to make a procedural change acts as an effective deterrent. The standard then acts as a roadblock to subsequent changes.

Quality standards don't guarantee that existing processes are the right processes. They encourage consistency rather than ongoing improvement and they ignore job structures that encourage positive employee behavior.

PRINCIPLE-BASED INDIVIDUAL CHANGE

We agree with the goals of a principle-based, individual change approach. Individuals influence their organizations and families by changing themselves. Integrity, honor, and trustworthiness should be the hallmark of every successful manager. I know of no business person who would not benefit by *applying* the techniques and perspectives introduced in this philosophy.

The problem with this approach lies not in its intent but in the lack of an adequate audience. This approach correctly states that intrinsic (or internal) motivation is the most powerful and that if this motivation is positive and honorable, significant change can result.

The difficulty is that most individuals within an organization are not interested in pursuing self-development. An interested few are sufficiently thoughtful, self-aware, and self-disciplined to be involved. We call these individuals *Value-Guided* because their actions are based on their own internal set of values. In most organizations, however, the rest of the employees are preoccupied with other issues. Their behavior is guided or shaped by their working environment or job structures. We call these individuals *Environment-Guided.* See Chapter 5—"If I Were You . . . " under the heading Motivation, for a complete explanation.

Even within the interested minority, most are open to self-development but are unable to *apply* the suggestions and make the changes. Most feel that by talking about the material, they have made the necessary changes (although people working in their departments may not agree).

This approach contains many excellent concepts, which I find helpful and challenging. The best of the principle-based material is the work done by Stephen R. Covey and his organization. While I wish that everyone could review personal motives, activities, and values as outlined in this approach, I believe the real audience for this material is management and primarily senior management.

Due to the limited audience and the lack of a process orientation, this approach is appropriate for personal change but lacks the practical tools most managers need.

Summary

Managers need equipment for the next activity-focused stage of improvement. The Improvement Toolbox provides a basic and practical understanding of how to forge a sustainable improvement effort using structure and uncomplicated tools. Understanding and applying The Improvement Toolbox will bring a significant return for any busy manager. The next chapter describes the format and design of The Improvement Toolbox.

2

How To Get The Most Out Of This Book

Method and Tools

WELCOME TO THE IMPROVEMENT TOOLBOX. This section will help you understand how the various chapters fit together into a complete unit.

Method Overview	1 - Introduction
	2 - How To Get The Most Out Of This Book
Method Chapters	3 - Why Most Improvement Programs Fail
	4 - The SMG Improvement Method
	5 - "If I Were You . . ."
Tool Overview	6 - Tool Collection
Management Chapters	7 - A Simple, Strategic Business Review
	8 - Creating The Business Case
	9 - The Reinforcing Structure™
	10 - Explaining Improvement Simply
Skills Chapters	11 - Six-Step Process Improvement Method
	12 - Service Improvement
	13 - Facilitating Improvement
	14 - Coaching
Research Overview	15 - Research Foundation

The Improvement Toolbox is arranged to allow you to quickly obtain benefit from the content and to help you apply the concepts in your organization.

The Improvement Toolbox is divided into two sections:

- Method Overview (the first half - the ideas *explained*)
- Tools Overview (the second half - the ideas *put to work*)

METHOD OVERVIEW - THE IDEAS *EXPLAINED*

The first five chapters comprise the *Method Overview*. Here the improvement method and the thinking behind it are described.

Chapter 1 - **Introduction**	We separate organizations into Stage 1 (Perspectives) or Stage 2 (Activities). Companies are looking for help in doing, not talking. Popular Stage 1 improvement programs are reviewed.
Chapter 2 - **How To Get The Most** **Out Of This Book**	The Method / Tools layout of the book is explained.
Chapter 3 - **Why Improvement** **Programs Fail**	The key attributes of a successful improvement effort are listed from our research with over 60 organizations. The four levers of the Reinforcing Structure™ are introduced. This information lays the groundwork for the SMG Improvement Method in Chapter 4.
Chapter 4 - **The SMG** **Improvement Method**	*The heart of The Improvement Toolbox.* First, a typical improvement experience is characterized and then the SMG Improvement Method is described step-by-step. An example of how to introduce change using the SMG Method is included.

Chapter 5 - **"If I Were You . . . "**	How to implement the SMG Improvement Method. **You'll meet the three different employee types. Every organization has them.** The three types explain why Stage 1 programs only work for a small group of people. The SMG Improvement Method addresses all employee types. Motivation is discussed and specific guidance is provided regarding steps and time frames for each management level.

TOOL OVERVIEW - THE IDEAS *PUT TO WORK*

The remaining chapters (Chapters 6 through 14) constitute the *Tool Overview*. The Tool Overview also subdivides into two main sections: Management Chapters and Skills Chapters.

- Chapter 6 - *Tool Collection,* describes the Tool Overview half of The Improvement Toolbox. Each of the remaining chapters is described with key points noted.

MANAGEMENT CHAPTERS

- Chapter 7 - *A Simple, Strategic Business Review,* provides a straight-forward, effective format for reviewing a company's strategic situation.

- Chapter 8 - *Creating the Business Case,* makes practical suggestions on how to present your organization's strategic situation to your employees.

- Chapter 9 - *The Reinforcing Structure™,* describes the four levers managers can employ to ensure that needed activities are completed and continue to be completed.

- Chapter 10 - *Explaining Improvement Simply,* introduces the Linear Progress Model™. This Stage 2 model describes the areas organizations are focusing on and the activities required for progress to occur.

SKILLS CHAPTERS

- Chapter 11 - *Six-Step Process Improvement Method,* can be applied to any business process. It easily equips you to define, document, streamline, and improve the steps or processes that add value in your company.

- Chapter 12 - *Service Improvement,* describes how customers think and the keys to delivering improved service and satisfied customers.

- Chapter 13 - *Facilitating Improvement,* covers the practical side of building an effective, personal facilitating style, including suggestions for meetings that work.

- Chapter 14 - *Coaching,* improves your ability to develop your staff with the nine principles covered here.

- Chapter 15 - *Research Foundation,* describes three major research projects that provided the foundation for the book.

CHAPTER REFERENCES

Chapters that describe specific tools or concepts are referenced. To ensure chapter referencing doesn't interfere with the flow of the text, the references are in short form—*(Chp. 9).*

READING THE IMPROVEMENT TOOLBOX

To quickly absorb the main points from The Improvement Toolbox, you should skim, then carefully read Chapters 3, 4, and 5.

Chapter 3 - *Why Improvement Programs Fail,* shows you what to avoid and introduces the Reinforcing Structure™ as the key to making changes sustainable. This chapter helps you to see the simplicity of the method described in Chapter Four.

Chapter 4 - ***The SMG Improvement Method*, is the most important chapter in The Improvement Toolbox.** It describes a technique that managers can use to build support for changes in the job structures of their staff. *The key to improvements that outlive the initial enthusiasm is to link changes with job structure support.*

Chapter 5 - *"If I Were You . . . ",* completes the description of the Improvement Method. Our motivation model covers three types of employees and explains why each type is covered by the SMG Improvement Method. Practical improvement strategies are listed (by management level and by scope) to guide your improvement effort.

3

Why Most Improvement Programs Fail

Setting the stage for the SMG Improvement Method

THIS CHAPTER DESCRIBES THE FOUR MAIN PROBLEM AREAS found in most improvement programs: Approach, Clarity, Productivity, and Sustainability.

- Approach problems arise when organizations poorly manage employee expectations and resources during a change.

- Clarity problems develop when organizations don't communicate simply.

- Productivity problems begin when organizations focus on getting more done rather than being more consistent.

- Sustainability problems occur when organizations neglect to install structures to encourage required behavior.

For each problem area, practical suggestions are given to help you avoid these difficulties in your organization. In addition, the structures you can use to help sustain behavior are described briefly at the end of the chapter (Reinforcing Structure™).

Obstacles To Change

Organizations want to improve performance; however, when trying to lift the anchors that hinder progress they run into snags. These obstacles take various forms including existing structures and organizational politics.

Existing structures can actively discourage needed change. In one situation, an award-winning printing company was losing money. Too many customer orders needed to be rerun, wasting material, frustrating customers, and wreaking havoc with production schedules. Senior managers traced the cause of the problem to the sales incentive. The sales commission system encouraged salespeople to obtain a few sketchy details before moving on to the next sales order rather than spend the time necessary to understand customer requirements. Past speeches aimed at improving the collection of critical information had no impact because of the power of the incentive system (or structure).

Organizational politics can be an obstacle. Some managers are willing volunteers. Others are conscripts. Sympathetic managers can adopt new methods enthusiastically, while other managers strongly resist. The uneven adoption among managers creates frustrated employees who must deal with conflicting perspectives. To obtain significant results, an organization must create job structures for managers to ensure even less-willing managers participate to a certain degree. The message of the Improvement Toolbox is to match desired activities with reinforcing elements that encourage the activities to continue.

Four Problems

Organizations introduce a variety of programs to encourage their employees to improve work activities. A number of organizations experience worthwhile gains, while at the same time, many struggle when introducing new activities. Many of the major obstacles organizations face can be grouped into four areas: Approach, Clarity, Productivity, and Sustainability. Each is briefly discussed to set the stage for the SMG Improvement Method described in the next chapter.

Approach

Our research tested a number of different factors concerning how organizations approach improvement activities. Organizations recorded significantly greater progress when their improvement efforts had the following characteristics:

- tangible management commitment;
- periodic, specific training;
- no visible launch;
- committed resources;
- patience;
- integration into day-to-day activities.

TANGIBLE MANAGEMENT COMMITMENT

Every article written on organizational change states that management commitment is the most significant success factor. In many organizations, however, management commitment is merely talk. Speeches exhort employees to perform additional tasks to improve performance. These tasks are placed on top of existing activities and survive until more urgent issues bump them from the top of the pile. The tasks cling to life as long as managers spend time prodding, nagging, and controlling. We call this *extraordinary* management attention.

Tangible management commitment, on the other hand, is action. Tangible management commitment involves changing job structures to encourage required employee behavior and to discourage contrary employee behavior *(Chp. 9)*. Employees look for definite changes, not talk, as the true test of management's commitment to an endeavor.

PERIODIC, SPECIFIC TRAINING

Organizations involved in our research recommended training people more often and more specifically. Typically, there is a flurry of training activity at the beginning of an initiative and no training scheduled later when employees are trying to apply the material. The organization is often disappointed when the planned results fail to materialize.

No one absorbs everything in one sitting; individuals learn at different rates and in different ways. People learn by linking and applying what they are learning to what they already know. Training should be scheduled over time and deal with job-related issues to provide support for the activity changes. Training is fully completed when organizations build motivation for the required activities into the work situation.

NO VISIBLE LAUNCH

Organizations that had a *visible* program start did not progress as well as those that started quietly. A visible program start could be defined as a high-profile, kickoff meeting accompanied by assorted items such as lapel buttons (with preprinted slogans), balloons, banners, and coffee mugs. The event is designed to create employee enthusiasm for the improvement program. Employees, however, see this event as part of the internal marketing of the effort. More talk, no action.

It appears a *visible* program start creates a target for the negative-minded staff to shoot at. Excited people promise things the organization cannot realistically deliver; employees don't see visible changes to support the effort; and cynicism builds. Organizations that quietly went about changing the work environment were more successful.

The answer is to build up a program slowly over time, being careful *not* to say things that raise expectations beyond what you and the organization can deliver. It is better to under-promise and then over-deliver. For example, if you promise more involvement in decision-making, you should change the managers' job structures to encourage this behavior *(Chp. 14)*.

COMMITTED RESOURCES

Organizations said they would commit sufficient resources to the improvement program rather than try to do it inexpensively. Many organizations eliminated needed follow-up training due to cost constraints. Others canceled training because of the cost of providing replacement workers for those involved.

A properly funded improvement effort can change key activities and generate substantial results. The benefits are worth the same resource planning that any other significant investment receives.

PATIENCE

Patience is a rare commodity. Most managers want to see an immediate turnaround in performance and morale. They want improvement and concrete results now! This is especially true for publicly held organizations where the pressure for short-term results can be so intense that even the most committed managers can be made to abandon long-term initiatives.

Organizations that looked for a less than one-year payback on their improvement effort did not progress as far as organizations with a longer-term perspective. Patience pays off. It takes time to build new activities into an organization.

INTEGRATION INTO DAY-TO-DAY ACTIVITIES

Improvements need to be integrated with normal day-to-day activities. Responding organizations that integrated their improvement focus into normal day-to-day activities did measurably better than organizations that considered improvement a special project. If improvement activities are mentioned only at quarterly meetings, then more pressing business concerns take their place. The Improvement Toolbox gives managers practical help in building ongoing changes into the daily fabric of their areas.

APPROACH SUMMARY

A successful approach involves management making specific changes to the measurements and structures that reinforce behavior. Employees are then able (due to training) and encouraged (because of changes in the job structures) to act differently.

Clarity

There are often communication problems in organizations involved in improvement. Managers use buzzwords to communicate common-sense ideas. Business people seem to have been infected by the *jargon* virus. This virus compels otherwise normal individuals to sound as if they swallowed the current top-10 business book list. Managers talk about paradigms, reengineering, empowering, and deploying, when they should talk about changing a model or perspective, organizing or redesigning, involving employees, and placing resources. Managers who like to be thought of as experts are vulnerable to this disease.

Rather than creating an understanding using a common vocabulary, specialized jargon creates barriers to understanding. The language (I could have said *semantics*) leaves a group that knows what the words mean, and another group that doesn't understand. Those who don't understand feel left out, or less intelligent. To avoid embarrassment, they stop participating. The company loses the benefit of this group's experience.

If your goal is to create an understanding and a sense of working together, simplify the language. Rather than tell employees you are looking to shift their paradigms, tell them you want to change how they view their work. Use visual explanations of the steps involved *(Chp. 10)*. If people understand, they can better translate concepts into action.

Productivity

Most organizations want to improve productivity. They cut costs hoping departments do more with less. However, the result can be a reduction in quality or customer service and no significant productivity gain. Why? To get more out in the same period of time, the people who remain *cut corners* to increase output. The corner cutting increases the inconsistencies (or variability) within the activities and decreases the quality of the product or service.

To increase productivity, you must reduce the *variability* (or improve the consistency) within a process. A business process is a series of steps or activities that produce an outcome for a customer or another department. In other words, work passes from group to group in a series (like a relay team) to produce an outcome.

Most organizations create product or service outputs using multiple-step processes and inconsistencies exist (however slightly) at each step. Since steps in the process follow one another, the variability affects the remaining steps, causing lower than expected output and quality.

The goal is to reduce variability at *every* step in the process and to reduce it *at the same time*. If you only focus on one or two steps and leave the rest, the variability remaining in the untouched steps still affects performance. Your improvement effort produces some benefits but not to the degree possible. If you eliminate inconsistencies at every step, you will see rapid and substantial benefits. The Improvement Toolbox includes a simple process improvement method *(Chp. 11)*.

Organizations must focus on consistency, not productivity. If an organization reduces variability within its key processes, improved productivity *and* customer service will result.

Sustainability

New ideas don't survive well in most organizations. Even great ideas that could result in significant improvement have a difficult time being absorbed into the day-to-day organizational machinery. Why? Organizations and individuals are resistant to change, but it is more than that. The way many organizations are configured almost defies attempts to improve or change. Other organizations rise above their peers with continued innovation and excellent performance.

As an example, consider theme parks or destination resorts. Most have high school and university students working part-time as frontline service providers. Most do an adequate job, but if you compare the standard of service experienced at a Disney resort with other smaller competitors, there is a difference. There is a standard of excellence about a Disney complex. From the cleanliness of the facilities to the knowledgeable, helpful and friendly staff, the difference continues year after year.

Disney may be bigger and better able to afford extensive training, but that doesn't explain the difference. In most people's minds, big organizations can't compete with smaller ones when it comes to providing specialized, customized service. People believe the larger an organization is, the more it forgets about individual customers.

Do the customers expect less because Disney is so big? No. Customers probably expect more because it *is* Disney. Are the students Disney hires smarter than the students working in other resorts? No. Disney's success is due in part to selective hiring, extensive training and jobs that are designed to encourage correct and sustained cast member behavior.

The training Disney provides to new cast members is comprehensive and focused on giving these individuals a sense of their participation in each visitor's experience. The job structures at Disney communicate in concrete terms the expectations the company has for its employees and ensures ongoing consistent behavior.

Perhaps your organization has very little in common with Disney, but most organizations are looking for ways to sustain improvement activities and deliver consistent, positive employee behavior.

A Solution With Four Elements

The key to sustainability is structure. Our research revealed that behavior, for the majority of employees, is shaped by the structures within their jobs *(Chp. 5)*. These job structures or the Reinforcing Structure™ as we call them, encourage specific activities and discourage other actions. A number of organizations understand this principle and use the same four elements included in the Reinforcing Structure™ to motivate employees to produce their best on a daily basis.

The Reinforcing Structure™

The Reinforcing Structure™ represents four major job structures *(Chp. 9)*: Organizational Structure; Performance Measures; Employee Evaluation Criteria; and Rewards and Incentives. Each element is covered briefly here to help you understand the SMG Improvement Method in the next chapter.

ORGANIZATIONAL STRUCTURE

The first element of the Reinforcing Structure™ is the organization's reporting structure or Organizational Structure. It is the way the organization determines how different departments, groups, and teams interact with the balance of the organization. Employees within a department tend to act in a way that reflects the priorities and goals of that department. Finance people tend to think and act like other finance people and sales people act like other sales people. While some of this is positive, other aspects of an organization's reporting structure can impede cooperation and progress.

One aspect of the Organizational Structure element is the degree to which the goals and objectives of the organization are reflected in the reporting structure. For example, if customer service is deemed important, then the department that represents customer concerns should be represented at a senior level in the organization's structure. By looking at the reporting structure, employees know how important an area is (or isn't).

The other aspect of the Organizational Structure element is the decision to structure around functions or processes. More companies are structuring along key processes to avoid interdepartmental conflicts over resources. Problems arise when needed resources are controlled by groups not directly responsible for the process or project.

The Organizational Structure element is a positive influence when the reporting structure is clear and matches the organization's goals, and individuals are motivated to cooperate in the organization's (not just their department's) best interests *(Chp. 9)*.

PERFORMANCE MEASURES

The second element of the Reinforcing Structure™ is the organization's use of performance measures. The way an organization evaluates the performance of a department, group, or team powerfully affects employee behavior.

One recognized municipality gauges the performance of its traffic department by using two measures: safety and throughput. By using both measures, the city creates a *balance* of behavior from the traffic department. If they were to only measure safety, the department might design intersections that sacrifice traffic flow for safety. If they only measured throughput, the department might sacrifice safety concerns to maximize the traffic flow rate. Together, both measures create appropriate department behavior.

Finding trade-offs is often the secret to performance that satisfies more than a single objective. Other examples of trade-offs are: long-term vs. short-term; departmental vs. organizational; business unit vs. corporate; quality vs. productivity.

The key is to evaluate what behavior is required from a department or group *as a part of the entire organization* and choose performance measures that reinforce appropriate behavior. By eliminating measures that fail to create positive behavior and installing new criteria to encourage needed activities, a manager can have a significant impact on the area's performance.

EMPLOYEE EVALUATION CRITERIA

The third element of the Reinforcing Structure™ is the organization's use of employee evaluation criteria. Just as group behavior is affected by performance measures, individual conduct is affected by employee evaluation criteria.

During the employee evaluation, you communicate the behavior the organization values and expects. The impact of the periodic evaluation can be positive, neutral, or negative. Why? If the evaluation covers crucial issues and describes in realistic terms the required behavior, then the impact can be positive. If the evaluation isn't linked to key activities and the description of the required behavior is incomplete or subjective, then the impression can be neutral or negative.

During a session with senior managers from a large organization, a discussion focused on how their managers were ineffective at a number of very important activities. Wishing to justify their behavior, one manager exclaimed, "Those activities don't happen because we are not held accountable for them." The managers' job structures didn't address the important activities. Until senior management notices and makes the necessary changes, the important activities will continue to be neglected.

Organizations should systematically review evaluation criteria. The evaluation process should include hard *and* soft skills (like coaching), describe specific behavior for each criterion, and contain consequences for positive and negative behavior.

REWARDS & INCENTIVES

These are the rewards, recognition, and financial incentives organizations use to influence employee behavior. They powerfully shape behavior and if well thought out, can improve performance.

Two years ago, the staff behavior at a local Seven-Eleven convenience store changed for the better. Each time I entered the store, I was immediately greeted with a cheerful "Good Morning." The appearance of the store also improved. Everything was tidy, clean, and well presented. When I paid, the clerk asked if there was anything else I needed. I was delighted.

Due to my experience in changing employee behavior, I wondered how long it would last. It lasted—without wavering. I continue to experience the same improved level of service although the individuals behind the counter change from time to time.

Once, after bringing my selection to the counter and experiencing a cheerful attempt to suggestive sell (or up-sell), I said "No thanks, but great job on the suggestive selling." I was not surprised by the clerk's response. The clerk said: "I never know when I am going to be *shopped* again."

Seven-Eleven pays employees to travel from store to store and pretend to be customers. These phantom shoppers buy merchandise and evaluate employee performance. If the shopper is greeted, the store meets predetermined standards for cleanliness, and the clerk suggests something to accompany the customer's purchase, then there is a financial reward—not two months later from head office, but immediately, on the counter. One clerk I spoke to confided he had received $150 over eight weeks, based on three visits. Since most clerks earn a little more than minimum wage, the award is significant. More significantly, it works. An idea to improve customer service resulted in sustained employee behavior, thanks to a well thought out training and incentive system.

What If You Don't Use The Reinforcing Structure™?

If the key to sustainable activity is structure, what could happen if the Reinforcing Structure™ wasn't considered before a suggested change was made. Here is a real-life example.

A telephone company wanted to improve customer loyalty. It determined the company's most frequent direct contact with customers was through their directory assistance lines. The company wanted this contact to be favorable to help retain customers.

The slogan they came up with was called "Own the customer's problem." The objective was to get customers the correct phone numbers even if they needed extra help with similar sounding last names or other issues. The "Own the customer's problem" strategy was rolled out for the telephone operators with great fanfare. Operators marched back to their desks convinced of their customer service value. The operators were intent on making phoning for directory assistance a pleasant experience, but because they were being paid on an incentive system for speed, their income dropped.

After two weeks, a national business magazine interviewed one of the supervisors. Her response was: "When we do what we're supposed to do, we are penalized for it."

Management forgot to consider the Reinforcing Structure™ already in place for the jobs in question. Telephone operators work in a very structured environment where supervisors make sure no time is wasted. The incentive system rewarded operators for spending as little time as possible on the phone as a way to encourage continued productivity.

This incentive system was in direct opposition to the "Own the customer's problem" strategy designed to improve customer satisfaction. As operators spent more time with customers, their pay checks decreased. Things went back to normal very quickly and the "Own the customer's problem" effort quickly became part of company folklore.

Why did it happen? It happened because the telephone company failed to ask the following question: *"What drives behavior in this environment?"* Had management understood what influenced the telephone operators' behavior, they could have matched the suggested change to the operators' environment.

The principle behind the Reinforcing Structure™ is that structural elements *create employee behavior.* The only way to see a lasting change in behavior is to change the structural elements.

The next chapter describes the SMG Improvement Method. This method avoids the pitfalls identified in this chapter and incorporates the Reinforcing Structure™ or job structures to ensure improved activities stay improved.

4

The SMG Improvement Method

Change — Structure — Success

THIS CHAPTER IS THE HEART OF THE IMPROVEMENT TOOLBOX. Whenever you have an improvement to make in your area, you can use the SMG Improvement Method to guide your steps.

The previous chapter focused on the four problem areas that hinder improvement implementation and introduced the four elements of the Reinforcing Structure™. The next chapter, *"If I Were You . . . ,"* explains the motivation model behind the SMG Improvement Method and discusses practical implementation issues you will face as you employ the SMG Improvement Method.

In this chapter, we describe the typical approach that organizations use to implement an improvement and compare it with the SMG Improvement Method. The steps involved in each approach are presented in slide-show sequence. The differences between the approaches are made plain in the Neat N' Tidy Car Rental example.

Management Levels and Time

If you are to understand the SMG approach, we must first review what happens in a typical organization when an improvement opportunity is recognized. The description is clearer if we separate the three levels of managers found in most organizations and lay out the steps in chronological order.

The working definitions for each management level follow:

SENIOR MANAGER

- The senior manager level controls the elements of the Reinforcing Structure™ such as the organizational structure, performance measures, employee evaluation method and rewards/incentives. This level usually develops the strategy for the organization.

MIDDLE MANAGER

- This management level often leads functional departments within the organization and provides support for those who oversee or supervise day-to-day work activities. This level has limited control over the elements of the Reinforcing Structure™. In some organizations, the middle management level is not present; in some organizations it can include several layers of management.

LINE MANAGER

- This level is responsible for overseeing day-to-day activities. In some organizations this level includes team leaders or supervisors. The focus is not on strategy and other planning-type issues but rather on getting the work out in the next few days or weeks.

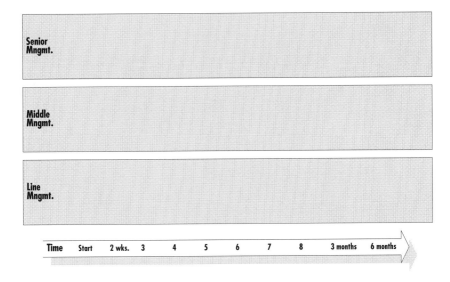

The diagram shows the three levels of management. The time-line arrow shows the period from the start of the improvement to six months later. This presentation of management levels and time allows us to picture the steps involved in implementing an improvement.

A Typical Improvement Method

The process starts when someone in the organization recognizes an opportunity for improvement. This individual recognizes the opportunity and pieces together a plan to implement the improvement. This recognition could be pictured like this:

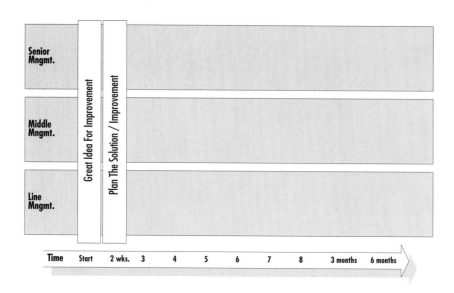

The great idea and the action plan development can originate from any level in the organization. The important thing is that the opportunity or problem *is* identified and a series of activities is planned to exploit the opportunity or to correct the problem.

Next comes an important step in any project or program—management commitment. The approval of those in charge is sought for the new initiative. This step could be pictured like this:

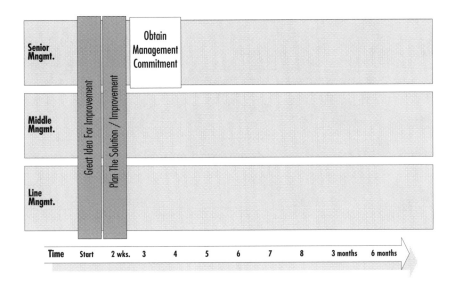

Contact is made with senior management. The objective is to obtain management's commitment to proceed. Several meetings may be necessary to lobby and convince senior management of the suggestion's value.

The commitment may take the form of a budget allocation or release of funds or resources. It may require the cooperation of other areas of the organization. It could result in a series of speeches being given by those in senior management to ensure cooperation and compliance.

Once senior management has agreed to the suggestion and resources required, the next step is to notify the middle managers (or administrative level) who control the affected areas of the organization. This notification is indicated on the model like this:

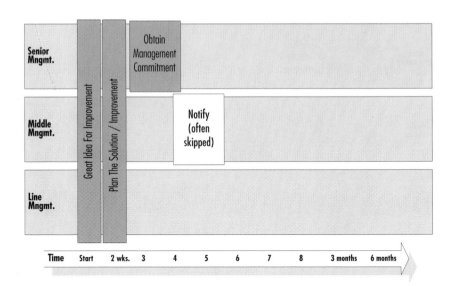

This step is skipped in many organizations. Since senior management has already given their blessing, the thought appears to be: "Why bother meeting separately with middle management since the need is so pressing. Just arrange a meeting with the actual line departments and send a copy of the meeting notice to the middle managers involved."

Middle management can be quite resistant to change. Often they wish to leave things as they are. A defensive reaction is understandable when changes are made to their area without consultation. We will assume the senior managers in this example recognize the value in obtaining the commitment of the middle managers and a meeting is held to notify them of the coming changes.

At this meeting, the middle managers ask some harmless questions (they learned long ago that asking too many pointed questions attracts a troublemaker image that severely limits future advancement). If any resistance to the suggested changes is offered, it is often subtle and after the start of the initiative.

Now for the real action. Our typical organization has seen the opportunity, worked on a solution, obtained senior management permission, and notified middle management; it is now ready to start with the actual implementation.

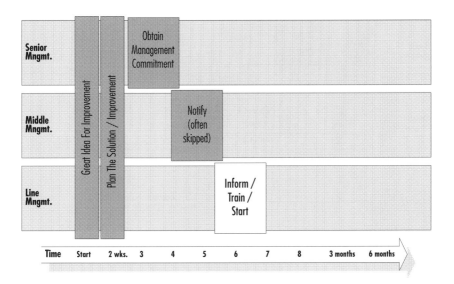

This step varies greatly in depth and duration. Some organizations only spend a few minutes discussing the reasons behind the change and what is expected of the individuals involved. Others go to significant lengths to ensure affected individuals understand the issues and mechanics involved in the change. While the depth of the explanation varies, most organizations inform and train the individuals involved and then initiate the required changes.

Things are looking up now. Action has been taken and initial results look encouraging, especially when interpreted by the group that suggested the change in the beginning. For a time, the affected departments give additional attention to the new tasks under the watchful eye of the sponsors of the suggestion. The staff accept the change and try to find time to put the ideas into practice.

A few weeks go by and it is time to measure the impact of the changes on current performance. Some organizations painstakingly measure the results of the effort, while others quickly pass over the area to ensure things look encouraging.

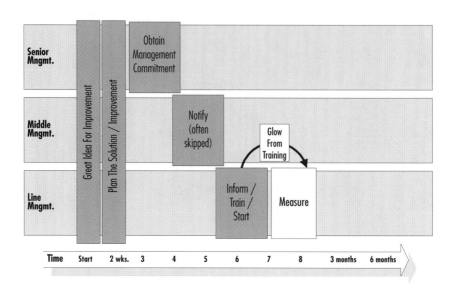

The evaluation may be too soon to be useful. The individuals are still enthusiastic and try to meet the new expectations placed on them. The enthusiasm and management attention (provided by the evaluation) are enough to ensure the activities continue for a few weeks. Senior management is informed of the initial improvement in performance. If we stop at this point, the change has been successful.

What happens next? Business is unpredictable and within a short period of time other issues arise that demand urgent attention. Perhaps a product or service under development runs into major difficulties or a major customer wants to see immediate changes. These urgent issues create their own sets of corrective activities and these new activities arrive on scene with "top priority" written all over them. It would be career-threatening to ignore these activities, so naturally they move to the top of the to-do list.

After several waves of activities caused by successive high-priority issues have washed over each department, individuals feel overloaded and react as best as they can.

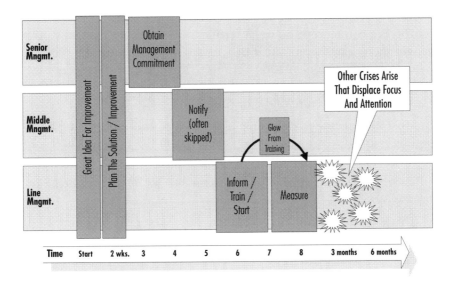

These crises have the combined effect of taking the organization's attention away from the change. More urgent problems create their own required activities and push aside the original improvement. The original suggestion fades away.

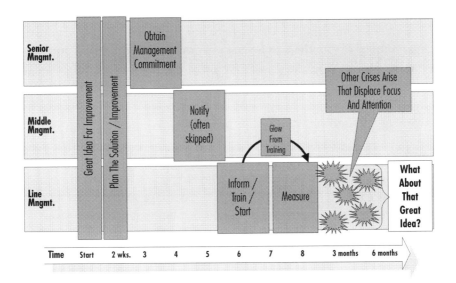

Later, those in the typical organization ask: "What ever happened to that great idea?" You may have asked yourself a similar question before.

This is a common response. A terrific idea is put forward that would benefit the organization, but it disappears. What's wrong? The idea is valid. Even the implementation approach, though important, is not the real problem. The key to sustainable activities is building the suggested change into the structure of the organization.

Most management programs assume that communicating compelling reasons to employees will accomplish the change. Their core notion is that convincing arguments and discussion modify behavior.

The reality is that explanation and discussion *do not* change behavior. Talking is not enough.

This is not a new message. Solomon, the wisest man who ever lived, spoke about this very issue in about 800 BC.

> *A servant cannot be corrected with mere words.*
> *Though he understands, he will not respond. (Proverbs*
> *29:19 NIV)*

In more contemporary terms, "Employee behavior cannot be changed with mere words. Though they understand, they will not respond."

Solomon says that getting people to act in a certain way requires action. Recognition, praise, appreciation, and warnings are examples of actions that motivate. Performance measures shape behavior, if consistently used. Behavior is also influenced by rewards and evaluation criteria. Department configuration affects behavior. Incentives shape behavior. Organizations obtain the employee behavior their structure encourages.

To be blunt, employees often do what they have to do, rather than what they should do. This is not the employees' fault. Since structure guides behavior for most employees, managers must build structures to encourage desired activities.

Some individuals naturally respond in exactly the manner that benefits their organizations. However, we have found most employees perform their activities in a way that minimizes difficulties and improves their situation. For example, sales commissions encourage salespeople to sell. Employees complete activities to obtain recognition, avoid criticism, or to feel a sense of accomplishment.

We are *not* suggesting all employees are motivated only by self-interest. We *are* saying that a realistic behavior model must include: those employees who are shaped by the work environment (the majority); those who perform well due to personal values; and those who seem to be motivated by other issues. Employee motivation is covered in the next chapter *(Chp. 5)*.

This is an intentionally simple but effective approach. **If you want employees to continue to perform in a certain way, then you must build motivation for the activities into their job structures.** Stage 2 organizations understand the link between structure and behavior.

Let's apply this structure thinking to the typical improvement approach and see the difference.

The SMG Improvement Method

As in the typical approach, an improvement opportunity is recognized by someone in the organization.

The difference here is in the planning of the proposed solution. The initiator should consider it only a draft plan, rather than try to fill in all the implementation details.

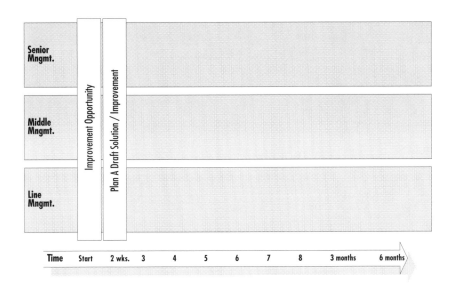

By showing others a draft version, you allow them to participate in the solution. You also demonstrate consideration for their views. The combination is effective. The resulting plan will be comprehensive, realistic, and supported by a wider group. The key is to talk *before* making the decisions.

I'm sure you've attended a meeting designed to obtain feedback on a proposed change, and once in the room, found the decisions were settled long before the meeting began. Those running the meeting didn't want your input because they had already thought of everything; the meeting was merely to notify those affected, including you. You left frustrated. Their disregard and lack of consideration moved you—away from the issue. The issue became *theirs* not *yours*.

By presenting a draft proposal, you show that you have respect for their opinions. Your actions demonstrate that you consider your own ideas a starting point, but understand different perspectives are required to ensure success. By presenting a draft, you encourage participation and spread ownership of the issue to others.

Senior management merely grants approval at this point in the typical approach. We recommend, however, a series of specific steps.

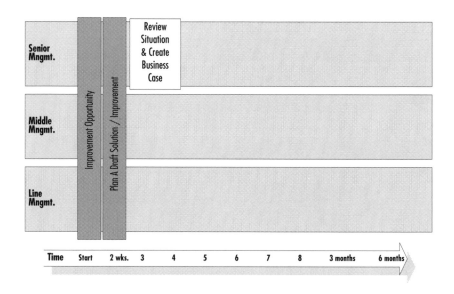

This step contains two tasks. Senior management's first task is to review the business situation to justify the improvement. Their second task is to explain the justification to the employees and managers.

This business situation review enables management to spell out the sound reasons behind the suggested improvement *(Chp. 7)*. If management periodically updates the review, this review process allows organizations to match strategy with specific activities, which is a key requirement of Stage 2 companies *(Chp. 1)*.

Once the review and justification are complete, the results must be explained to both managers and employees in clear, uncomplicated terms. This presentation or business case explains your organization's current situation and why the improvement is important. The point is not to simplify things so much that you insult the intelligence of your prospective audience, but to explain your reasoning, using nontechnical language to communicate the essential points *(Chp. 8)*.

This combination review/presentation has a number of benefits:

- Management has a straightforward tool to link strategy and activities.

- Employees understand that there are objective business reasons behind the improvement (rather than only a manager's opinion).

- Employees are taught about the business and begin to understand and appreciate the decisions being made by management.

- Employees are more willing to modify their activities and commit themselves to a change they understand.

Senior management should grant any necessary budget approvals or permissions to allow the improvement to be implemented. These approvals alone are not sufficient to ensure a successful outcome. Senior management must also structure jobs to create the motivation for continuing activities.

To accomplish this, senior management must start by identifying required changes to employee and managerial behavior. For example, middle management may need to change their monitoring activities or provide additional training. Employees may have to include additional activities or change existing ones. Consider all affected groups to see whether different behavior or activities are necessary. Some groups may need to change their behavior to adapt to the improved method. Identify exactly what changes in behavior will be required.

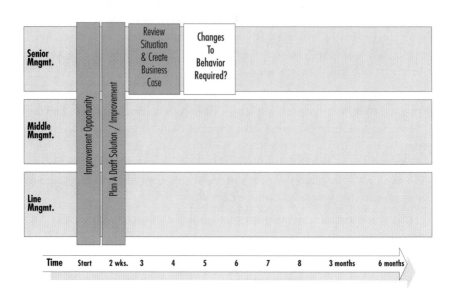

The next step is the most important in the SMG Improvement Method. Consider each employee or managerial group separately and for each group ask yourself: *"What drives behavior in this situation?"*

You must identify the structural elements that encourage typical behavior. For example, is a group's performance gauged on a specific measure? Are individuals evaluated by performance targets like sales quotas? Are incentives given for meeting objectives? Are departments encouraged to cooperate or are individual departments measured on their unique priorities? This analysis takes only a few minutes but saves a lot of frustration.

Then you must draw up job structure changes to reinforce the behavior the improvement requires *(Chp. 9)*. The suggested job structure changes are assembled in draft form for future discussions with the affected groups.

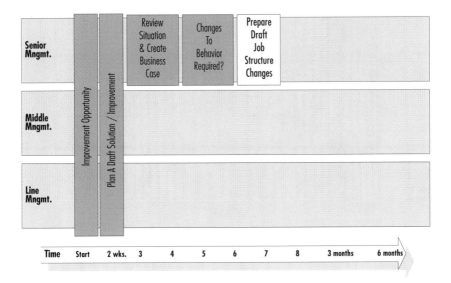

To save time, draft job structure changes can be prepared while middle and line management sessions are conducted. These steps will be introduced in a moment.

While you can adjust the steps to fit your situation, we have found that the described sequence is the most effective way to introduce an improvement.

Senior management has reviewed the business situation and compiled the justification in an understandable business case to present to the organization. They have considered the changes in employee and manager behavior required to make the improvement successful. They have also looked at what drives current behavior among the affected groups and whether any changes would be required in the job structures to create lasting employee motivation. These prospective changes have been compiled.

The action now moves to the middle management level. This level does not control job structures or the Reinforcing Structure™, but it is responsible for supporting the decisions and directives from above and ensuring that appropriate activities continue.

The objective is to bring the middle management group on-side *before* the improvement is implemented.

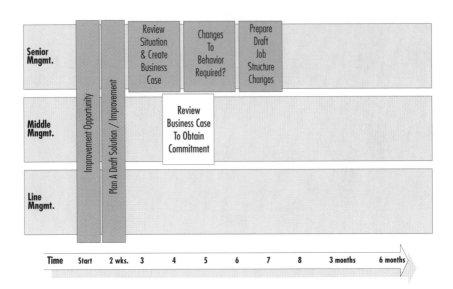

Here you discuss the business case with middle management. By reviewing the business reasons for the improvement, middle managers can broaden their perspectives and provide valuable feedback. Helping them see the wider picture is important. Frequently, departments are measured on their specific contribution rather than on their participation in the organization's success. As a result, their focus becomes narrow. Departments become concerned with optimizing their measures and lose sight of organizational goals.

In one high-technology organization, customers are now given a bigger voice and their rapidly changing needs are causing significant changes in the operation. In a recent employee survey, the organization asked whether individuals thought changes were being implemented quickly enough to keep customers happy. The results of the survey revealed the different perspective middle managers often have. The survey showed people at both the top and bottom of the organizational chart thought changes weren't happening quickly enough. Those in the middle thought the changes were happening far *too* quickly and they thought the company was in danger of losing control.

When middle managers are evaluated based on their departments' activities, some try to strictly control employees to improve their departments' measured performance. Giving employees more influence over their activities can be perceived by the managers as a loss of control. To counteract this tendency, senior management must communicate the business reasons for involving employees and create job structures that encourage middle managers to bring employees into the management of day-to-day activities.

Other benefits of discussing the business reasons are:

- People feel more comfortable with change if they are involved beforehand.

- Middle managers can edit your business case to ensure it is realistic and understandable for their employees.

The next step is to discuss middle managers' support activities in light of the improvement and see if any changes are required. Any change to your job can be threatening, so preparing middle managers for upcoming changes minimizes any negative reaction.

If you match specific changes with related training, the changes will be less troubling. For example, if you expect middle managers to lead a cross-functional team, you should provide a session on how to facilitate team meetings.

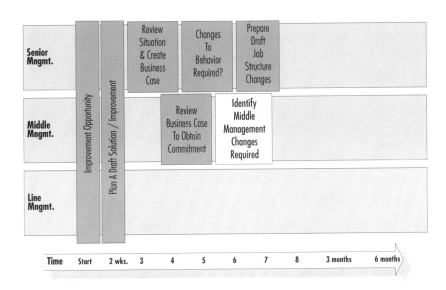

We now move to the line level of the organization. The first step is to review the business case with them.

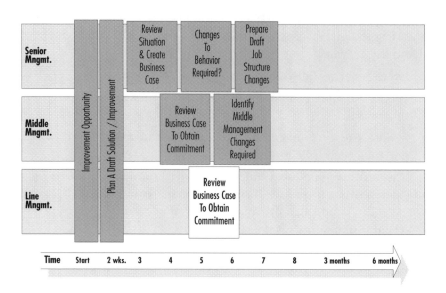

| | | | Review Situation & Create Business Case | Changes To Behavior Required? | Prepare Draft Job Structure Changes | | | | | |
| Senior Mngmt. | | | | | | | | | | |

(Vertical labels between columns: Improvement Opportunity / Plan A Draft Solution / Improvement)

| Middle Mngmt. | | | | Review Business Case To Obtain Commitment | Identify Middle Management Changes Required | | | | | |

| Line Mngmt. | | | | Review Business Case To Obtain Commitment | | | | | | |

| Time | Start | 2 wks. | 3 | 4 | 5 | 6 | 7 | 8 | 3 months | 6 months |

Present the business case to line management and staff to encourage personal commitment to the improvement. This helps them understand the broader business reasons behind the change and allows them to make suggestions based on practical experience.

Their reaction will be positive. It is often the first time anyone has attempted to make the business objectives and necessary activities clear to employees. They frequently comment that they never understood how all the pieces fit together until now. Previous management announcements were like individual pieces of a puzzle without the picture on the box. They now see the overall business situation and even begin to appreciate recent management decisions.

The benefits of showing line management and employees the business case are:

- increased employee esteem because of the time taken to explain background information;
- a sense that their opinions have value within the organization (or at least within this improvement effort);
- less resistance to change due to explaining the reasons before making adjustments;
- feedback from a credible source – people who actually do the work.

The next step is to conduct required training and equipping sessions to allow employees to perform the improvement activities.

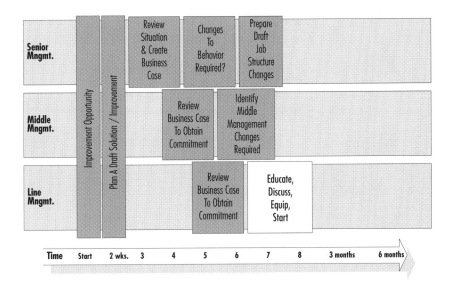

These sessions should include:

- an explanation of improvement that links vision and activities *(Chp. 10)*;

- training on how to describe a process and how to solve problems *(Chp. 11)*.

Although many other training companies teach material intended to accomplish the same objectives, SMG's research found that the material currently being taught by these organizations was not put into practice by the majority of their trainees. Those trained found the material impractical and too complex. SMG discovered that only simple models and easy-to-use tools are adopted by trainees and used on a regular basis.

After the education and training is completed (following the guide included in The Improvement Toolbox) employees understand why the change is required and what should be done. They are equipped with the necessary tools and can go back to their work areas to get started.

Senior management's participation in the improvement is not over, since the improvement has not yet been built into the structure of the organization. Senior management must discuss with both middle and line management levels the previously prepared job structure changes.

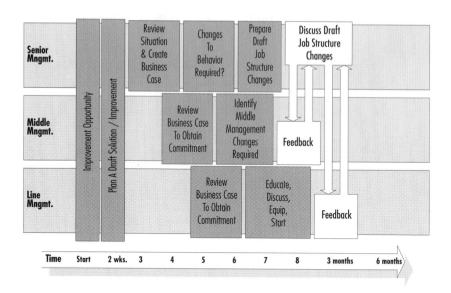

We say *discuss* not *decree*. In some organizations, senior managers are not used to asking for feedback; they expect *confirmation,* then *compliance.* This is a very important and critical phase in the implementation. We are not suggesting organizations become pure democracies where every decision comes by the will of the people. We believe business owners have the right to make decisions that are in the best interest of the shareholders.

However, if managers want employees to act more responsibly, they must be willing to ask for feedback when appropriate. To quote Glenn Carroll, a noted communication specialist: "People don't resist change, people resist *being* changed." Even if the changes are straightforward and the justification appears to be plain to all, managers and companies reap significant returns by investing time in sincere discussion.

The discussion of the job structure changes should include a brief overview of why the improvement is necessary and what behaviors must be adjusted to sustain the improvement. Discuss the various ways these behaviors can be encouraged *(Chp. 9).* Let employees ask questions and think about the specifics for a short time.

The objective is to encourage required behavior. Employees may suggest a different recipe for motivating the desired activities. Explain to employees that the formula you agree to should encourage the behavior, while not causing other performance problems.

If this step is rushed (beyond what the situation requires) or if the dialogue is superficial, it will appear to be an attempt at coercion. However, if the pace matches the situation's urgency and the exchange is sincere, there will be a positive outcome for all concerned. This interaction could take a couple of days or up to a number of weeks, depending on the situation's complexity.

It is the responsibility of senior management to ensure this interaction is successful. Senior management has a chance to build a job environment that drives ongoing, positive behavior; the initiative is worth the effort.

The SMG Improvement Method is a technique that managers will use each time they make a change. Managers, over time, will become proficient at identifying the rewards, employee evaluation opportunities, and performance measures that create desired behavior.

Mission statements are useful for instilling values and core ideals, but *reinforcement drives behavior*.

Once the discussion has been concluded, senior management communicates and implements the job structure changes. Depending on the types of changes required, this could take from an afternoon for a simple change to up to a year for a complex change such as reworking a sales compensation system.

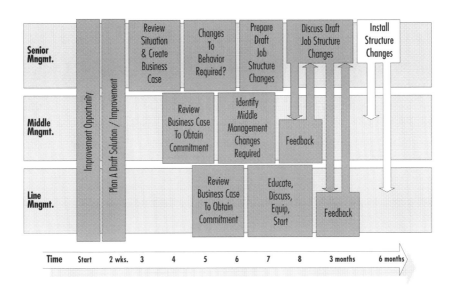

The improvement is now implemented and its associated activities are consistently being carried out because of the motivation in each individual's job structure. You cannot guarantee ongoing behavior by educating and equipping employees. You can, however, ensure that an improvement becomes part of the daily routine rather than a fond memory by building in the necessary motivation.

The completed model now looks like this:

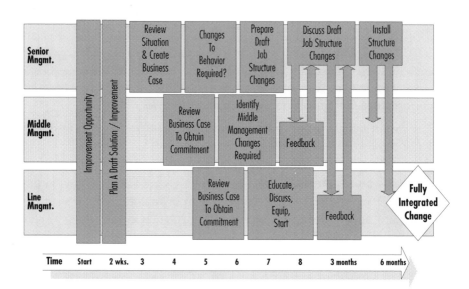

The improvement activities have now been fully integrated into the organization's daily work.

That explains the SMG improvement method. Now let's look at a situation and see how the SMG improvement method can reduce management workload and improve area performance.

An Example From A Manager's Perspective

My lifetime goal to own and run a business is within my grasp because of a recent inheritance. I purchased a set of airport car-rental agencies called Neat N' Tidy Car Rentals. Neat N' Tidy was losing money and the founder wanted to retire, so I obtained the business at a good price. I figure with my leadership anything is possible, even breaking even! I survey the three offices in the three regional airports to decide what I should do first.

The first thing I notice is that my counter fronts don't look as clean and crisp as those of my competitors'. Some of the older national rental agencies are quite run down, but Neat N' Tidy is in the middle as far as appearance goes. The operations manager is doing an excellent job of keeping the cars clean and ensuring billing goes smoothly.

I decide to spend a little money where the customers will notice it. I get the Neat N' Tidy logo redone and arrange with a painter to give the three office counters a fresh coat of corporate color. I leave to spend a few days in accounting, reviewing the books and trying to increase Neat N' Tidy's line of credit.

I inspect the offices again. The new paint is great, but the actual counter tops are often cluttered with old rental agreements and other miscellaneous items. I look at each office's copier and computer terminals; they look as if they had never been cleaned. I guess Neat N' Tidy's staff never considered cleaning as part of their job. Each airport's cleaning company cleans the floors and empties the wastebaskets. The clutter and dirty office equipment detract from the Neat N' Tidy image. The back end of the operation is clean enough but I think the customer's first impression is important. I decide it is time to act.

The improvement opportunity is in our company image. The initial customer impression should match the company name. I need to ensure that the counter tops stay clear, everything else is clean, and things are stored in a tidy fashion.

APPROACH 1 — TYPICAL

Since I'm the owner, I don't have to get anyone's permission to proceed. I inform the staff that I don't think the appearance is up to the level it must be to stay competitive. I tell them about the connection between being competitive and being able to employ people. I also say that I expect staff to be responsible for ensuring the counter is cleared after each customer is served and the office equipment and other visible items are clean and neat. I tell them that I know sometimes it gets busy and some customers are a pain, but customers pay the bills. There are a few questions regarding the specific expectations (how clean is clean?) and I thank them for their time and continued cooperation. While going to the next office, I begin to feel a sense of deja vu about my talk. I have heard many managers give similar presentations. I hope mine leads to more action than those speeches caused. I supply some soft rags and a bottle of glass cleaner to each location.

All appears solved. For two weeks each counter is spotless; ten years of fingerprints have come off the office equipment. Then a billing problem surfaces and demands my attention. A government change means every invoice for the last six months must be pulled to determine if customers rented cars while on government business. All government business must be logged, totaled by month and submitted monthly. After a month's work, we get the invoices pulled and the report submitted.

A week after the government invoice situation settles down, two of my senior staff leave and I have to find, hire, and train two new office managers. More time goes by.

Three months later, I do another inspection tour. More clutter and fingerprints are visible. The staff have forgotten about the cleanliness drive of a few months back. I provide additional encouragement by way of a loud pep talk. I could scream and yell on a regular basis, and that may work for a time, but I want to be sure this is consistently part of *the way we do what we do*. Our appearance is important to our corporate image, but my periodic pep talks are not effective in creating a long-term change.

APPROACH 2 - THE SMG IMPROVEMENT METHOD

The same situation exists, but I decide to use the SMG Improvement Method to integrate the cleanliness requirement into Neat N' Tidy's regular activities.

Since I am the only senior manager in the operation, I sit down and plan my approach. For my business review, I put together a little presentation about appearance for my staff. I take some photographs of other rental counters and fasten them on a piece of cardboard. Below each picture, I write the market share percentage for the company involved as well as their growth rate. Finally, I indicate whether or not the company is making money. The visual survey works out well; the most clean counters belong to the most successful companies. I can't wait to show my staff, but first I must consider the behavior changes that are necessary and what elements of the Reinforcing Structure™ could be used to reinforce the required activities.

The behavior change I need to see will add a small amount of cleaning and discipline to the customer service job. When I think about what *drives* behavior for my customer service staff, I don't really know. There is a yearly evaluation, but since my staff are young, there is a high turnover as people move on to other jobs. I guess the yearly evaluation doesn't really shape customer service behavior.

If the rental agreement isn't filled out properly, the operations manager makes sure the customer service staff remember their error. As a result, the rental agreements are handled fairly well. The office managers emphasize courteous and friendly behavior with their customer service staff, and since they are right there to observe daily activities, the staff are usually friendly and helpful. I had to conclude there wasn't anything in the customer service job that created the motivation to keep things Neat N' Tidy.

There are a number of alternatives I could use to create motivation for the customer service staff. Using the four levers of the Reinforcing Structure™ *(Chp. 9)* as a guide, I list some of my options.

ORGANIZATIONAL STRUCTURE:

- The organization is flat: I am the only senior manager; there is an operations manager, and three office managers. I decide the structure of the organization is not a problem.

PERFORMANCE MEASURES

- I could create a cleanliness standard and every time I visit I could rate the location, graph the results from all three locations, and post the combined chart in each location.

- I could create a checklist or schedule for periodic cleaning during the day and have customer service staff initial beside each cleaning. These checklists could be handed in to me each week. If I wanted to be severe, I could even say that if the checklists were not handed in, the payroll would be delayed until I received them. Perhaps that would send the wrong message to the staff and work against the participative climate I'm trying to instill.

- I could modify the rental paperwork and create a customer feedback section. I could entice customers to fill it out by monthly drawing the name of a customer and giving away a free car rental. The survey would give me a running gauge of each location's cleanliness and other key issues. I could post the results of the surveys in each location. Administering the program and reprinting all the contracts would be a lot of effort and cost. I wanted to *reduce* my workload, not add to it.

EMPLOYEE EVALUATION CRITERIA:

- Staff turnover works against me. We have a very informal evaluation method for staff who stay longer than a year. I decide to include a section on cleanliness and neatness. However, since many staff never see the evaluation, I decide it's too infrequently done to create the motivation for this type of behavior.

REWARDS AND INCENTIVES:

- I think of doing an Employee of the Month recognition award like some of the other rental companies. But in some of those companies the same picture gets put up month after month. Either they have stopped changing the picture or their method only picks their best employee. My objective is to motivate all my employees to do their jobs better, rather than just encourage one or two staff. I want to change the customer service staff's perspective. They should consider cleanliness as an integral part of their job.

- I could give surprise inspections and present a cash award to all customer service staff on duty, but I have difficulty paying staff to do something I think should be part of their job. This method may work well in large organizations, but I don't have the resources to pay any extra for clean counters. They don't need to spend extra time; they could straighten up while waiting for the next customer.

- I could introduce a variable-pay system and make 10% of their wages dependent on the results of the customer satisfaction survey. That would do two things. It would create strong motivation for the employee. It would also create a monstrous headache for me. The accountant is already pulling out hair over the complexity of the pay system and the other changes I have made since taking over the company. How could I ensure surveys were evenly done by all locations and in a balanced manner? I decide the number of returned surveys would be too small to ensure an even picture of a single location's performance. The idea has merit but I couldn't handle the increased complexity right now. Perhaps I could in a few years.

THE MEETINGS

I call a meeting of three office managers and the operations manager. I show them my cardboard presentation on cleanliness vs. profit. I explain that the best performing companies have the best appearance. I point out the relationship between a company making money and potential raises. They catch on quickly.

We also discuss the various options to motivate the staff to clean regularly. I ask for their advice. They recommend the checklist be handed in on a weekly basis but without the payroll penalty. They feel the checklist would make cleaning a normal part of the customer service function. I agree, but ask them how they are going to ensure things *continue* being done.

We finally agree that all the managers should include the completed checklists in their weekly reports. I will be evaluating each manager periodically and the timely completion of their weekly summary reports will be considered. The managers understand the checklists are now a part of everyday life, if they want a raise in the future. I ask the four managers to create a draft checklist form and give them a week to complete the draft.

A week later, I have a meeting with the staff at each location. I show all the staff—customer service and operations—my cardboard presentation. I picked up a few things from my presentation to the managers and I include them now. The presentation goes well. They understand cleanliness is important to the success of the company. Each office manager presents staff with the draft checklist the managers worked on. I ask staff members to look at the form and offer any suggestions they feel would make it better. I give them a week to edit the form before we get it printed and start the new activities.

I'm glad I asked for their input. The resulting form is more comprehensive than I first envisioned. It now has a section for up-front counter issues and another section covering the operations—car return issues. Another side benefit comes to light. The cleanliness issue has become a staff issue, where it was only mine before.

The best part is that I personally don't have to do anything more to keep the cleanliness focus alive. Now the job structure is going to do that work for me. I could get used to this.

Summary

This simple example shows that by modifying your improvement approach and by building the necessary motivation into the job structure, you can help your organization encourage positive behavior.

Once you go through the method in a few situations, it will become quite natural for you. It will transform the way you view the change process, so you can't be content with the typical method.

5

"If I Were You . . . "

Motivation + Picking the Right Strategy

THE DESCRIPTION OF THE SMG IMPROVEMENT METHOD is completed in this chapter. Chapter 3 describes four common problems and keys to a successful improvement effort. It introduces the Reinforcing Structure™ as a way to ensure that desired activities continue in your organization. Chapter 4 contrasts the steps in a typical improvement effort with those in the SMG Improvement Method. The Neat N' Tidy example illustrates how a manager can use the method to build an improvement objective into the organization's structure.

The purpose of this chapter is to:

- explain the motivation model that underlies the SMG Improvement Method;
- provide implementation outlines for most improvement situations.

The motivation model shows you how to recognize the three different types of employees and describes each type's response to change. The chapter details three improvement strategies and three levels of management. Choose a strategy that fits your objectives and management level, and use the outline to guide your implementation. The chapter ends with a summary of activities that make up the SMG Improvement Method and a list of critical issues to help you as you plan your improvement effort.

Motivation

The SMG Improvement Method and all the improvement strategies described in this chapter share the same motivational model. This simple model contains the three steps needed to change behavior and involves:

1. Explaining the business situation *(internal motivation)*
2. Understanding and simple tools
3. Changing job structures *(external motivation)*

The SMG Improvement Method *(Chp. 4)* uses these three steps to encourage change at the middle management and line management levels. In this chapter, however, the motivation model behind the method is revealed.

It is the same for a line manager, a middle manager, a senior manager, a vice-president, or an owner of an organization. This framework is the secret to building a successful improvement (or change) effort. The three-step motivation model described above can be divided into two components:

UNDERSTANDING + SIMPLE TOOLS

Teach simple and effective techniques to help employees improve and manage activities *(Chp. 10, 11, 12)*.

MOTIVATION: INTERNAL + EXTERNAL

Use *internal motivation*—the business case presentation *(Chp. 7, 8)* and *external motivation*— job structure changes *(Chp. 9)* to encourage activities to continue.

The business case is shown to employees to encourage personal commitment to the change (internal motivation). Next comes the education or training step (understanding + simple skills), and then job structures are adjusted to encourage needed activities (external motivation). They combine to make a *motivation sandwich*.

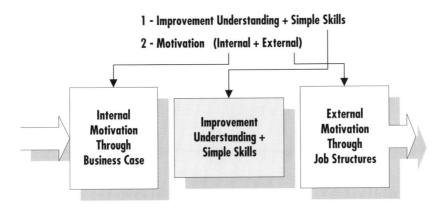

Motivation Sandwich

These steps describe the key elements to any successful change. But why should we discuss internal and external motivation separately? Don't all employees need the same steps?

Yes, but for different reasons. The business case alone is enough to convince *some* employees to change their behavior. For other employees, the business case is just the start. Those employees need more substantial motivation.

The SMG Improvement Method works because it accommodates all three types of employees.

THREE EMPLOYEE TYPES

We have found, as you have, that all employees are not the same. Employees can be classified in one of three types:

- Value-Guided;
- Environment-Guided;
- Not-So-Guided.

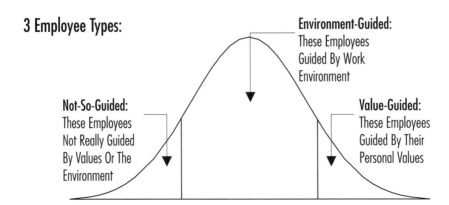

3 Employee Types:

Environment-Guided: These Employees Guided By Work Environment

Not-So-Guided: These Employees Not Really Guided By Values Or The Environment

Value-Guided: These Employees Guided By Their Personal Values

VALUE-GUIDED EMPLOYEES

There are employees who always seem to perform well in their positions. They are responsible, customer-oriented and loyal. They react well to changes, as though they had been waiting for the adjustment to happen. Managers say: "If we only had a few more employees like . . . ., this department would be terrific." Let's call this employee type—Value-Guided.

These employees are controlled more by their personal guidance systems than by their jobs. Their refreshing nature is evident the first day they walk through the organization's front door. They are outstanding employees—with a great attitude. Their performance, however, is not due to outstanding coaching. These employees continue to perform well with few external influences.

Many organizations want their Value-Guided employees to lead other employee types in improvement efforts. Value-Guided employees can be frustrated by other employees' lack of intensity.

ENVIRONMENT-GUIDED EMPLOYEES

The majority of employees within a typical organization are Environment-Guided. These employees are influenced or guided more by the organization and people around them than by personal factors. Environment-Guided employees perform well in the right setting, but in a negative situation, they go along with the majority.

It is often easier to shape a new plant culture in a new facility than to reshape established behavior in an existing company. This is due to the effect of established job structures on Environment-Guided employees.

When people are hired they generally accept the new philosophy and try to fit in. It is much more difficult to overcome history, tradition and entrenched patterns of relating.

These employees are not moved by vision and mission statements. Their behavior is primarily influenced by the environment in which they find themselves.

NOT-SO-GUIDED EMPLOYEES

In many organizations, there is a small minority who do not fit easily into the other two categories. Their behavior doesn't seem to be guided by a personal standard of excellence or the environment in where they find themselves. Perhaps they are guided by negative personal factors (such as a need for attention or control), rather than positive ones. The good news is that this group is in the minority. If you do not pay more attention to them than their numbers deserve, they will not have a serious impact on your improvement effort.

Our advice: spend your time and energy on the other two types and virtually ignore this group. By trying to win them over, you give them more attention than they deserve and reward their behavior. This increases their perceived power and encourages contrary behavior to obtain additional attention and influence.

The SMG Improvement Method — Internal and External Motivation

To motivate an individual to change behavior, you must encourage specific activities in the working environment and give employees an opportunity to hear and understand the reasons for the change. The SMG Improvement Method provides both.

INTERNAL MOTIVATION

Internal motivation is provided through the business case that describes why the improvement is important. This business case comes from a review of your organization's business situation *(Chp. 7)*. The information is compiled in simple terms and presented to your employees to help them understand the reasons you are pursuing the improvement *(Chp. 8)*.

Why do the various employee types need to hear and see the business case presentation?

Value-Guided employees need this information to adjust their personal value systems. The behavior of these employees is based on personal values and their perception of their company's best interest. By making adjustments they can continue to act in a positive manner. You can often change their activities simply by communicating new information.

Environment-Guided employees need to hear the justification for the improvement to believe the reasons behind the change are legitimate rather than arbitrary. The information alone is not sufficient to change their behavior, but it does clears any potential roadblocks for the second step in the motivation process.

Not-So-Guided employees should hear the business case or justification so they are treated equally with other employees. The information will not have a significant effect upon their behavior.

The following diagram shows the types of employees within your organization and why the internal motivation step is so important.

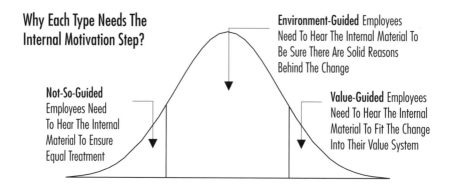

Why Each Type Needs The Internal Motivation Step?

Environment-Guided Employees Need To Hear The Internal Material To Be Sure There Are Solid Reasons Behind The Change

Not-So-Guided Employees Need To Hear The Internal Material To Ensure Equal Treatment

Value-Guided Employees Need To Hear The Internal Material To Fit The Change Into Their Value System

EXTERNAL MOTIVATION

What is External Motivation? It is consciously changing the employees' job structures to ensure behavior is consistent with the organization's best interests.

This may sound like manipulation. It is, but in a positive sense. We are not suggesting that organizations take advantage of their employees. We *are* suggesting that within a moral, ethical and health-conscious setting, organizations build job structures that encourage positive behavior to continue. This is not coercion. It is a way of providing a better outcome for the employee who performs more closely to the model of behavior that the organization has identified as optimum. It is a means of ensuring that good behavior is encouraged and poor behavior is either not encouraged or is actively discouraged.

A good example of external motivation is the practice of using phantom shoppers to secretly test retailers' customer service employees. Seven-Eleven and Nordstrom successfully use this technique. The possibility that a phantom shopper may appear and reward correct customer service behavior provides encouragement for consistent conduct. Disney uses an extensive training, monitoring and recognition program to ensure that their employees (cast members) present the same courteous face, day after day, and year after year.

External motivation creates job structures (the four elements of the Reinforcing Structure™) to encourage positive behavior *(Chp. 9)*.

Why do employees need to have their job structures changed to support specific activities?

Value-Guided employees want job structures that demonstrate the organization's commitment and reinforce their goals. This type of employee doesn't rely on job structures for motivation, but sees the changes as necessary follow-up to the improvement effort. Value-Guided employees respect an organization with complementary goals and job structures.

Environment-Guided employees need changes to the job structures to motivate them to change their behavior. Their behavior is shaped by the setting they find themselves in, so adjusting the setting is the way to encourage changes in their behavior. The Environment-Guided employees have been waiting for job structure changes ever since the business case was presented to them. Words are OK, but these employees feel that a capable organization acts to back up its intentions.

Not-So-Guided employees need changes to the job structures to motivate them to *think* about changing their behavior. As the rest of the organization moves off into the sunset, these employees see the inevitable and slowly move toward the model of desired behavior being encouraged by the job structures. They never fully adopt the model, but the job structures have entrenched the new philosophy so that there is nothing they can do about it.

The following diagram describes why the External Motivation step is important to each employee type.

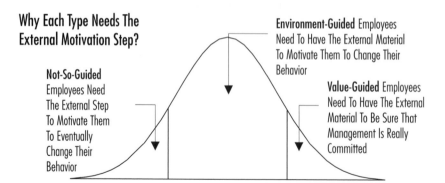

Why Each Type Needs The External Motivation Step?

Not-So-Guided Employees Need The External Step To Motivate Them To Eventually Change Their Behavior

Environment-Guided Employees Need To Have The External Material To Motivate Them To Change Their Behavior

Value-Guided Employees Need To Have The External Material To Be Sure That Management Is Really Committed

No matter where you are in your organization and no matter what your objective, you need internal and external motivation to successfully create long-lasting change. You also need to teach employees simple, effective techniques so they can make actual improvements.

Picking The Right Strategy

This section describes three management levels and three strategies for implementing improvement. Since many managers will read only the segments that apply to their situation, some repetition is included.

The section proceeds in the following order:

- description of management levels;
- description of three improvement strategies—Departmental, Inter-Departmental, and Organizational;
- guidance on the choice of strategy;
- outlines for each strategy by management level;
- summary.

As a general rule, your position in the organization determines what you can accomplish and how quickly it can be done. Senior managers exercise considerable control over the organization and the structures that motivate employee behavior. As a result, they can introduce change more widely and more quickly than middle or line managers.

We do *not* believe that less senior managers should give up because they do not personally control all of the tools within the Reinforcing Structure™. We have seen middle and line managers make significant changes within their organizations.

In one example, a middle manager improved the culture and morale of a small company. He involved employees in many areas that were previously controlled by management. After one and a half years, employees made the final hiring decisions, decided the pay grade of new positions, and scheduled the operation to maximize the sales volume. It was an impressive transformation.

Line managers can also powerfully influence the organization even if they don't control all of it. Positive changes made within a single department can create a desire for similar change in other areas.

Line managers may not control the ways their areas are measured by senior management. By adding specific performance measures and minimizing others, however, it is possible to create motivation. Performance measures are powerful behavior modifiers and can be shaped by a line manager who seeks to encourage improvement behavior. By monitoring performance measures in daily and weekly meetings and posting the department's results, line managers incorporate measures into the daily routine; they can also shield staff from less positive performance measures, minimizing their negative effect. The built-in performance measures encourage effective behavior.

Three Management Levels — Three Improvement Strategies

You must answer two questions before you determine which of the three improvement strategies is best for your situation.

The first question is:

What level of management reflects my present position?

The second question is:

What do I want to accomplish?

The second question could be also be: "How quickly are results required within the organization and how broad is the area that requires the improvement effort?"

Management Levels

To help you answer the first question, the following definitions include senior, middle, and line management. These three roles summarize management activity in most organizations.

The management definitions are more concerned with what managers control rather than what activities they perform. Organizations without middle managers will be able to implement the SMG Improvement Method equally well. Please see the following definitions for each level of management.

SENIOR MANAGEMENT

Senior managers are near the top of their company's organization chart. They may be the owners of the company or members of the group of managers who report to the owner or controlling board. Senior management's responsibility is to create the context or environment that supports both the strategic direction and the improvement activities that ensure success. This means that as a senior manager, you control the makeup of departments, the criteria they use to measure group performance, the manner in which the organization evaluates individual performance, and the way individuals or teams are rewarded for their contribution.

These four areas comprise the four elements of the Reinforcing Structure™: the **Organizational Structure**, which is the reporting structure and the way the assembled departments reflect the goals of the company; the **Performance Measures,** that are applied to various departments and key activities; the **Employee Evaluation Criteria,** by which the employee's contribution is measured; and the **Rewards and Incentives,** which are intended to motivate employees to act in a pro-company manner.

Through these structures, a senior manager can shape an organization and its activities. This does not mean that senior managers have unlimited control; in fact, they may be frustrated about a perceived lack of control. As more and more organizations move to a more team-based management model, the management team is increasingly likely to discuss important decisions among themselves before action is taken. Senior managers then control the four elements of the Reinforcing Structure™ with other members of the senior management team.

MIDDLE MANAGEMENT

Middle managers are responsible for supporting and encouraging the employees' daily activities. They often have more than one department or business process to oversee. Middle managers generally do not control the context or the elements of the Reinforcing Structure™. This means that most middle managers have little power to change the way the organization is structured. They can provide potential justification for such changes, but someone else must make the final decision. They have some control over choosing performance measures to evaluate their groups' achievements.

In reality, performance measures have more impact on behavior if they originate from higher levels of management. There is a danger that performance measures introduced by middle managers may be pushed aside by measures originating from a higher management level.

Middle managers generally have some control over the format of the employee evaluation criteria and method of evaluation. They supply specific performance-related information for the year but the overall method and format is often dictated by a higher management level. Senior managers often install the procedures that calculate rewards and incentives. Middle managers are asked for specific performance and employee information and along with line managers determine the employees who qualify for recognition and rewards.

LINE MANAGERS (OR SUPERVISORS)

Line managers are responsible for managing one or more processes within an organization. Their interests focus on day-to-day management of their specific areas. Their objective is to improve consistency and performance; they provide direct guidance to those performing the work of the organization.

Three Improvement Strategies

There are three strategies or degrees of involvement that will be discussed. Each outline can guide a manager through important steps that can lead to a successful change. While all the outlines or strategies employ the same philosophy or framework, each deals with a different degree of involvement, from focused and narrow to broad organization-wide involvement.

The *Departmental* strategy is intended to improve the performance of a small, focused area (usually a department). The *Inter-Departmental* strategy is the next step up and is designed to help a manager with an improvement focus covering a process that spans a number of departments or areas, but not the entire organization. The *Organizational* strategy is an outline for introducing the improvement effort throughout an entire facility or organization.

While all three use the same core method, there are differences in the objective, scope and time involved. The differences are listed here:

DEPARTMENTAL

Objective:	Narrow	To improve the performance of a specific process or single area.
Scope:	Narrow	Looking in detail at a single process or problem.
Time:	Short	A few weeks to a few months.

INTER-DEPARTMENTAL

Objective:	Focused	To improve the performance of a cross-functional process or a problem affecting a number of areas within the organization.
Scope:	Medium	Looking in detail at an area or process that crosses departmental boundaries.
Time:	Medium	Approximately three to nine months.

ORGANIZATIONAL

Objective:	General	To improve the performance of an entire facility or organization.
Scope:	Broad	Looking to improve key processes and employee behavior within the organization.
Time:	Long	Approximately one to two years.

Choosing A Strategy

It is important to realize that the strategies are not mutually exclusive. Your organization could employ two or even all three strategies at the same time. If appropriate, you could also start in one small area of the organization to quickly improve its performance, then move to an Inter-Departmental or Organizational strategy once senior management recognized the benefits and value obtained. All three strategies are effective because they are based on the SMG Improvement Method.

If you are a senior manager, you can choose from any of the strategies. If there is a specific process or area that needs attention, select the Departmental strategy. It is the best choice for a rapid change in a specific area. If you want to tackle a cross-functional process, select the Inter-Departmental strategy. It can bring people together to improve the core process(es) involved. If the entire organization needs to improve performance to better serve your customers or clients, then the Organizational strategy is the best choice.

A middle manager can choose initially from either the Departmental or Inter-Departmental strategies. The Organizational strategy requires power and control that is usually the domain of senior management. A middle manager can sell senior management on a broader effort, especially after there are tangible signs of improvement in your area.

Line managers or supervisors can choose the Departmental strategy to improve the performance of their areas. The other two strategies require that other managers get involved with the effort and as a group you would implement a strategy.

The following table describes the reasons why managers select particular strategies.

Departmental	Inter-Dept.	Organizational
To improve the performance of a single area or process.	To improve the performance of a cross-functional process or solve a problem.	To improve the performance of an entire facility or organization.

3 Strategies - 3 Levels -		What approach is available to:	
Line Managers	There is a requirement for improved performance in the manager's immediate area. This is possible because the manager controls the area.	Not available initially. The line manager must convince other managers to cooperate toward a common objective as the solution is outside his/her own area.	Not available initially. The line manager must convince senior management that a wide-spread improvement program is required.
Middle Managers	There is a requirement for improved performance in a specific area or process under the manager's control.	There is a requirement for improved performance within the manager's control. If outside, then other managers must become involved.	Not available initially. The manager must convince senior management that a wide-spread improvement program is required.
Senior Managers	There is a requirement for improved performance in a specific area or single-department process.	There is a requirement for improved performance in a broader area or cross-functional process.	There is a requirement for improved performance in the entire facility or organization.

Strategy Outlines

Each strategy is described in three parts, which correspond to the motivation sandwich framework mentioned earlier:

1 - Internal motivation (through the business case)

2 - Improvement understanding and simple skills

3 - External motivation (through job structure changes)

The implementation of internal and external motivation depends on your management level.

Departmental Strategy

The departmental improvement strategy targets a specific area or process within the organization. For a localized problem or process that needs immediate attention, the departmental strategy is perfect. This strategy yields relatively quick results (in one to three months). Since the scope is quite narrow, there is usually only one manager involved. While this strategy is available to the line, middle, or senior manager, there are differences in how the strategy is implemented.

INTERNAL MOTIVATION

The first step is to provide internal motivation for the individuals in the department. Present the business reasons for the improvement to the employees involved to help them understand. Employees should see that what they are doing is important and that the reasons behind the proposed changes are clear and not *arbitrary*.

We help them understand *why* we are doing something. Often they hear *what* they should be doing and the *why* is glossed over. By spending the time to explain the reasons, you demonstrate respect and appreciation, and give the employees an opportunity to develop a personal commitment to the outcomes that you are talking about *(Chp. 7, 8)*.

For the line manager:

Create a simple analysis of your organization's business situation as it relates to the planned improvement. A small situation often does not need a full-blown business case. Gather the necessary information on customer/client requirements and try to obtain some measurable objectives that the improvement effort could target. This also applies to situations where the customers are internal departments or individuals rather than external customers.

For the middle manager:

During your analysis of the business situation, capture information relevant to the target department and its activities. Describe the direct customer benefits of implementing the improvement and the gains the organization would achieve in return (e.g., better customer retention or satisfaction). Remind employees of the relationship between organizational performance and job security. Businesses cannot guarantee job security, but employees should recognize the link between exceeding customer expectations and remaining in business.

Include the area's line manager in your investigation and analysis. Develop and present the business case with the help of the line manager to demonstrate management cooperation and unity.

For the senior manager:

Everything mentioned above under middle manager is also appropriate for the senior manager. By including the lower managers in the analysis and presentation, you prevent a backlash by managers and assure initial cooperation. Refrain from presenting an organization-wide improvement justification unless it is presented very simply and relates strongly to the activities and performance of the specific department. If you are too broad in your presentation, you will create undue confusion and a loss of focus on the department.

IMPROVEMENT UNDERSTANDING AND SIMPLE SKILLS

You have helped the department in question to see *why* their performance should improve. Now it is time to help them understand the essentials of improvement and to equip them with some simple skills so that they can make the necessary changes *(Chp. 10, 11, 12)*.

Some managers, eager to improve performance, want to skip the improvement explanation and jump right into the process improvement tools. We understand the desire to save time and the temptation to move immediately to fix the problems. We do not, however, recommend the shortcut. We have found that merely showing people the improvement tools doesn't create the desire or the understanding to use them properly. In our experience, the best balance is to make understanding improvement at least 50% of the training time with the other half going to learning and practicing the improvement tools on specific problems.

EXTERNAL MOTIVATION

The employees have now been exposed to your insightful and relevant analysis of the organization's business situation; they understand the basics of improvement; they have learned and practiced the improvement tools. You are now ready to begin the last step in the motivation sandwich.

Once you create external motivation for the improvement activities using the job structures, there will be ongoing pressure to continue required actions. Your management level determines the degree and number of job structures you can access.

For the line manager:

Line managers *can* usually manipulate the performance measures affecting their departments. They typically *cannot* change to a significant degree the structure of the organization, employee evaluation criteria, or the rewards and incentives that affect their employees. For this reason, line managers tailor specific performance measures to encourage positive behavior. Line managers can add new measures that encourage key elements of the needed improvement. Checklists are effective tools for line managers looking to increase consistency. As employees complete the required activity, a checklist can be filled out and returned to the supervisor or manager *(Chp. 9)*.

For the middle or senior manager:

Like line managers, middle managers *can* usually manipulate the performance measures affecting target areas. They can make minor changes to the organizational structure of specific departments. Middle managers can change the organizational structure of the target department although this is usually not done in a Departmental Strategy because structure changes normally involve more than just the target area.

Middle managers do not normally control the employee evaluation criteria or the rewards and incentives that affect their staff. Both employee evaluation criteria and the rewards and incentive elements of the Reinforcing Structure™ are broad instruments and, as a result, are not used in the Departmental Strategy.

Senior managers have access to all the elements of the Reinforcing Structure™ but to influence the performance of a target department, they should use performance measures, which can be set up quickly and designed to reinforce precisely the right behavior *(Chp. 9)*.

Inter-Departmental Strategy

The Inter-Departmental Strategy is the best choice for a manager wishing to improve a cross-functional business process or tackle a problem that encompasses a number of areas within the organization. This strategy expands on the Departmental Strategy encompassing more people, time, and effort. Communication is key to the success of the Inter-Departmental Strategy. All the affected areas and the senior managers must be informed and consulted during the process. In fact, you will find that the amount of communication required increases as the scope of the strategy broadens.

As in the Departmental Strategy, the same format or framework is used. You must teach simple, effective techniques to employees as well as create motivation, through internal and external means.

INTERNAL MOTIVATION

This strategy requires a more comprehensive look at the organization and the importance of the improvements than is needed in the Departmental Strategy. We want to go further in developing a clear picture of the implications for the organization. This may mean that your analysis of the business situation produces a financial justification for budget, equipment, or assignment changes *(Chp. 7)*. From the analysis, you can create a business case, describing the reasons clearly to the employees to encourage their personal commitment to the improvements *(Chp. 8)*.

For the line manager:

The Inter-Departmental Strategy is not within the line manager's direct control. To initiate an improvement effort in a broader area or a cross-functional process, a line manager must obtain commitment from all the affected managers (including middle managers). A coalition of the affected managers must be formed to coordinate the process. This means first convincing the middle and senior managers that the improvement is needed (usually not difficult) and that changes must be made to support the improvement behavior (more difficult). Buy them copies of this book to help them understand the improvement process. If all else fails, tell them that it was originally their idea and you are merely following through on their inspiration.

For the middle manager:

There are two possibilities here. In scenario one, you control the entire area you want to work on, including all the departments involved in the cross-functional process. If this is so, consider yourself fortunate. Normally, however, this is not the case. In the other more common scenario, you only control a portion of the area or process that needs improving. In North America, most organizations still identify departments by their function. This means that you will be working with other middle managers to accomplish your objective.

You will understand why some don't see the entire situation as you do if you recognize that other managers' priorities are different from your own. Walk them through the issues you discovered during the analysis. Be careful not to preach, but rather lay out the facts and ask their opinion on the implications for action.

Work through the analysis of the business situation with the other middle and line managers and put together the business case for the employees. If necessary, justify any additional resources from senior management. Time spent keeping other managers informed and positive is never wasted time. If you keep others involved, you will avoid many difficulties when unexpected changes come. Involved people are more willing to adapt and assist. Keeping them informed should take a sizable portion of your time.

For the senior manager:

The senior manager must include the affected subordinate managers in the business review, business case creation, and the presentation to employees. Resist the urge to jump too quickly to the conclusions. You risk losing your managers and then the effort becomes *your* project. As a senior manager, you are used to taking information, analyzing it quickly, and moving to action. Your people are probably not used to it.

The key to making improvement activities happen is to get employees involved *(Chp. 10)*. Getting employees and managers involved and thinking takes time. Allow them to discover and try the improvement method for themselves and encourage them to repeat it every time they need to change activities. This is the real objective: developing people who can think, react, analyze, and make changes without your moment-by-moment attention. Only in this way do organizations truly leverage their human resources.

IMPROVEMENT UNDERSTANDING AND SIMPLE SKILLS

You have communicated to employees *why* the area's performance should improve. Now it is time to help them understand the essentials of im provement and equip them with some simple skills so that they can make the necessary changes.

In the Inter-Departmental Strategy, there is usually a key business process at the core. This process spans a number of areas, but it must be dealt with as a single, integrated process. Having each department improve their portion of the process will not produce the expected performance improvement. I recommend that you bring representatives from each area involved in the process together in a temporary team. Teach this team the content described in Chapters 10 through 12. Have them apply the process improvement skills on the business process; then make sure team members carry the findings and recommendations developed by the team to their own groups.

EXTERNAL MOTIVATION

Finally, you need to create external motivation through the job structures of the managers and employees. In this way, the organization provides ongoing motivation for employees to continue to improve performance.

For the line manager:

To participate in the Inter-Departmental Strategy, the line manager puts together a coalition of managers to guide the improvement process. The component of the Reinforcing Structure™ that is most effective here is the Performance Measures element. The other elements are usually not available to line managers because of their broader impact on the organization.

Performance measures should be selected to monitor the improvement in the cross-functional process. By measuring each individual area involved in the process by the performance of the whole process, you can create motivation to cooperate and communicate. Individual areas only see performance improvement by working together.

For the middle manager:

If you are fortunate enough to control the entire cross-functional process being targeted, things will be easier. Go through the elements of the Reinforcing Structure™ to determine which combination will provide appropriate encouragement. Since the entire business process is under your control, you could change the Organizational Structure to improve the way areas interact and cooperate. Leave time for changes to the Organizational Structure to settle. Performance Measures may be a better element, if you want to move quickly. By changing the Employee Evaluation Criteria, you will reinforce positive behavior over time. Rewards and Incentives should not be implemented for a year or two, until the improvement is well entrenched. Only then will you be able to determine the behavioral implications of introducing a particular reward or incentive.

For middle managers who don't have the entire area within their control, the advice above still applies. Work with other middle managers involved to select appropriate elements from the Reinforcing Structure™ to encourage improvement behavior.

Middle managers often do not control the organizational structure of the departments involved. It is possible for middle managers to select (or influence the selection of) performance measures for their areas. It may be necessary to remove (or reduce the impact of) performance measures that only look at departmental issues, or do not encourage improvement behavior. These measures should be replaced by ones that encourage process-wide performance. This encourages cooperative behavior and minimizes departmental barriers.

Middle managers usually do not control the Employee Evaluation process and often find the process to be less than effective. Most middle managers feel that the process doesn't evaluate or encourage the behaviors required for success (e.g., personal work ethic, problem solving ability, or customer orientation). Middle managers occasionally influence the selection of evaluation criteria, but often they use a form designed for common use. One manager avoided this problem by writing only the bare essentials in the corporate office-configured portion of the evaluation form. She used a custom insert that evaluated the specific behaviors the department needed.

Rewards and Incentives are usually not within middle management's control. However, middle managers should look at existing reward, recognition or incentive policies and ask: "What behavior is encouraged by this policy or practice?" If the effect of the measure is not positive (as in a situation where a reward is given for increasing volume output, but increases in warranty charges or customer returns are not considered), the policy's mixed signals should be brought to senior management's attention. Include your ideas for correcting the measure (e.g., modifying the reward to include penalties for returns or warranty charges).

For the senior manager:

There is a danger of the senior manager moving more quickly than the situation deserves and legislating the required changes. If the changes are needed immediately and concern the organization's survival, make the changes. The objective behind the SMG Improvement Method, how ever, is to get managers and employees thinking about improving performance on an ongoing basis. I recommend that you develop some draft changes to the elements of the Reinforcing Structure™ and discuss them with the middle and line managers involved in the cross-functional process. Once you have discussed the prospective changes with them (not just informed them), then you can make your decisions and roll out the changes that will encourage appropriate managerial and employee behavior.

You may need to change middle management coaching or support behavior to facilitate improvement activities. If you are the only senior manager involved, then change activities as necessary. If the supporting activities are dictated by other senior managers, you can lobby for modifications.

By training staff to perform important tasks, managers bolster employee self-worth and gain increased capability. Employees will generally meet the expectations placed on them, whether positive or negative. The moral: Keep your expectations high and your people will rise to meet them.

INTER-DEPARTMENTAL SUGGESTIONS

Time should be given to the representatives from each department to define, describe and improve the processes they share. After the processes are defined and streamlined, a senior manager should encourage each area to implement a Departmental Strategy. Each department should then evaluate the activities and information it provides to the rest of the organization. The consistency and performance of these activities should be improved to complete the improvement approach.

For example, an organization has a business process that crosses three functional departments. An organization would:

1. select representatives from each department;
2. explain the business situation and what needs to be improved;
3. teach the representatives improvement basics and the six-step process improvement method;
4. encourage the team to improve process performance;
5. modify job structures to motivate ongoing activity.

The result is a defined and continually improving process. The next step is to go to each of the three departments involved, and complete steps 2 through 5. Each department's job is to improve the delivery, con

-sistency and performance of the information, products or services it provides to the rest of the organization, especially those it contributes to the business process being reviewed.

In summary, the Inter-Departmental strategy identifies what must be done, and done well, across an entire business process. The Departmental strategy focuses on what a specific department provides to the business process and how this contribution can be improved. If both approaches are employed, the performance of the process and cooperation between the areas improves dramatically. If changes are made to the managers' and employees' job structures, then the improvement continues and the benefits of the effort continue. If the job structure changes are not made, then the improvement activities fade and the effort never realizes its potential.

The Organizational Strategy

This strategy is for the owner, senior manager, or director who wants to improve the focus and performance of the entire organization. This approach is broader than either of the previously mentioned strategies. The Organizational Strategy involves more people, more departments, and more processes. Correspondingly, more time is required and there is a greater emphasis on the Reinforcing Structure™. By removing contrary structures and installing positive elements, senior managers can create an organizational climate that continues to produce both outstanding results and encourage greater commitment from employees.

The Organizational Strategy requires more communication than the other two strategies. Though they may find the process frustrating, managers who keep the lines of communication open throughout the change avoid difficulties.

The same motivation framework also applies to the Organizational Strategy. The objective is to create a motivation sandwich to encourage lasting change.

Develop the improvement opportunity as a draft outline. Review the business situation to confirm strategic goals and check assumptions. Summarize the analysis and the justification in a business case to explain the objectives that must be reached and why they make sense. This supplies internal motivation by helping employees understand the reasons for the improvement *(Chp. 7, 8)*.

Resist the urge to manipulate the facts to create a crisis. A fabrication can undermine the fuel of your organization's potential—trust. If the straight facts don't create a compelling reason for the suggested changes, then they may be seen by staff as arbitrary. In every case we have been involved in, the facts gave abundant justification for improvement and change.

Some may protest that insufficient profits do not justify substantial changes. We disagree. A for-profit organization is responsible not only to customers and employees, but also to shareholders. We find it beneficial to explain to employees that shareholders are looking for average or above average returns, just as employees look for good returns on their retirement savings investments. We remind employees that for-profit organizations that do not generate sufficient revenue lack funds for development (to keep them competitive) and training (to keep employees marketable and effective).

Next, provide understanding and train employees in simple improvement skills *(Chp. 10, 11, 12)*.

Senior management must discuss (not dictate) the draft changes to existing job structures for both middle management and employees. This is a crucial step. The discussion is separate for each level. It must cover senior management's appraisal of current behavior and the behavior changes needed to support the upcoming improvement. After listening to the feedback from each level, senior management can modify the planned job structure changes. The changes may not be substantial, but any changes are an indication that you value their opinions and are prepared to heed their advice.

Once the proposed job structure changes are agreed upon, they can be rolled out over time to provide the external motivation for the improvement *(Chp. 9)*. This ensures that improvement activities become daily activities. Because things are improving, you now have time to develop your best managers *(Chp. 14)*.

Of the companies studied by our firm, the best (or Stage 2) organizations followed a similar model for changing activities and improving processes. Some senior managers instinctively observed steps similar to the SMG Improvement Method. Because it came naturally, many could not explain the steps to their subordinates. The Improvement Toolbox makes the required steps clear and accessible to every manager.

The correct perspective is to target *major* processes, one at a time, over a period of time. Reduce inconsistencies and improve performance in each process, then move down to the departments involved. Help each department deliver their output to the main process as consistently and efficiently as possible. Reinforce needed behavior by modifying the job structures of those involved. As you reach further and further down into your organization, the impact will be significant. It may take six months to two years, but the long-term impact is worth the effort.

Summary

SMG IMPROVEMENT METHOD ACTIVITY LIST

1. Identify an improvement opportunity and prepare a draft implementation plan that describes what must be done, what resources are required and the desired outcomes.

2. Review the business situation and describe why the improvement is necessary *(Chp. 7)*.

3. Summarize the business case or the justification for the improvement in light of the business situation *(Chp. 8)*.

4. Consider the behavior required to make the improvement successful. What drives employee behavior now in the affected areas? Are job structures creating motivation to continue improvement behavior? Prepare draft changes in the job structures of those involved *(Chp. 9)*.

5. Review the business case with middle management to create an understanding that will lead to personal commitment to the objectives. Discuss how the presentation can be made clearer, simpler and more concise for line level employees. Is there a lot of jargon?

6. Discuss whether there must be any changes to the way middle managers provide support to the line level. Middle managers should be equipped to facilitate and coach improvement activities *(Chp. 13, 14)*.

7. Review the business case with employees to create understanding and personal commitment. For some employees, this will be the first time that anyone has explained how the business works and how much their behavior matters.

8. Hold education and training sessions to show employees that ongoing improvement is essential for continued success as a company *(Chp. 10)*.

9. Show employees how to improve a business or service process. Help them to apply their understanding to existing processes and to make required changes *(Chp. 11, 12)*.

10. Discuss the draft job structure changes that you prepared earlier. Make a sincere effort to allow some flexibility in format. You should discover that their suggestions improve the result and bring valid issues to light. Give them a reasonable period of time to consider the prospective changes and understand how they will help to ensure success.

11. Roll out the job structure changes after receiving their feedback. The time required will depend entirely on the complexity of the change. It is much easier to implement a checklist than to change an entire compensation system for a sales force. When you are done, however, you will have taken a significant step toward building an integrated, improvement-focused organization.

CRITICAL ISSUES

REINFORCING STRUCTURE™ EQUALS CHANGE

Structures motivate behavior. Many problems are caused by an inappropriate Reinforcing Structure™ that reinforces negative conduct. By changing the mechanisms that drive behavior, you will present employees with a reasoned, integrated approach, rather than a quick-fix reaction to a problem. Employees have been looking for these changes all along. By building motivation using job structures, you assure that support continues and activities are sustained.

EXPLAIN WHY

Show employees the business reasons for the change. Are they due to competitive pressures, customer changes, or shifts in the marketplace or technology? By showing the business case behind the changes, you help employees see the effort as less arbitrary. In this way, you help employees support and internalize the change.

PATIENCE

A healthy dose of realism and patience is required. Expect positive results, but also recognize that problems that have taken years to develop will take a while to mend and heal.

DON'T OVERPROMOTE OR OVERSELL

A slow and quiet start accompanied by structure changes is better than a loud beginning. The big bang theory is not a good model for organizational change. Be wary of hard marketing with banners, mugs, buttons, balloons and promises that create unrealistic employee expectations that management can't satisfy.

PACE THE EFFORT

The proper model is the marathon, not the sprint. It takes time to create a working environment that reinforces positive behavior.

DEVOTE RESOURCES

Devote resources to the effort. Identify and keep the potential benefits constantly before management. Tangible results are a big help, too.

KEEP LANGUAGE CLEAR & SIMPLE

Clear, simple communication is essential. Most improvement communication is seasoned heavily with jargon. The objective is to make people understand and adopt the change, rather than show employees complicated models that cause confusion. If you can't explain the objective, approach and benefit easily on one page, then it's too complicated. Your objective is to create a plain, common vocabulary to describe improvement principles and activities in your organization.

DAILY, DAILY, DAILY

Don't add to the pile. The objective is to encourage daily activities rather than a flurry of preparation for a quarterly meeting.

ELIMINATE VARIABILITY

Variability seriously affects the performance of a business process. Common wisdom recommends that you focus initially on a process step that can be rapidly improved. But concentrating on one step does little to improve the performance of the entire process. Treat the entire process as a whole; reduce variability at every step; and you will see significant results.

6

Tool Collection
Essential Tools For Managers

TOOL OVERVIEW

THIS CHAPTER DESCRIBES THE TOOLS outlined in the second half of the book. Chapters 7 through 10 explain the steps involved in the management side of the SMG Improvement Method. Chapters 11 through 14 describe specific techniques to involve your employees in improvement activities.

Method Overview		1 - Introduction
		2 - How To Get The Most Out Of This Book
	Method Chapters	3 - Why Most Improvement Programs Fail
		4 - The SMG Improvement Method
		5 - "If I Were You . . . "
Tool Overview		6 - Tool Collection
	Management Chapters	7 - A Simple, Strategic Business Review
		8 - Creating The Business Case
		9 - The Reinforcing Structure™
		10 - Explaining Improvement Simply
	Skills Chapters	11 - Six-Step Process Improvement Method
		12 - Service Improvement
		13 - Facilitating Improvement
		14 - Coaching
Research Overview		15 - Research Foundation

Management Chapters

**Chapter 7 -
A Simple, Strategic
Business Review**

Helps summarize the key points concerning your business situation and your current goals. Gaps between the two become opportunities for improvement. Takes a day the first time through. Updates can be quickly done (quarterly if desired). Brief, but powerful. A Stage 2 tool to link strategy and activities.

**Chapter 8 -
Creating The
Business Case**

Hints on how to take the results of your business review and turn them into something your employees will understand and appreciate. A key to real employee involvement.

**Chapter 9 -
The Reinforcing
Structure™**

The four elements are covered in detail with specific recommendations on how to create job structures that will encourage employees to keep doing what the company needs them to do. An essential instrument for Stage 2 organizations.

**Chapter 10 -
Explaining
Improvement Simply**

The Linear Progress Model™ is a perfect example of the Stage 2 activity focus. Three improvement dimensions summarize company vision and required activities. Easy to understand. As a diagnostic tool, it shows employees where your organization is and what you must do to proceed. The model educates and explains how to move to the next stage.

Skills Chapters

**Chapter 11 -
Six-Step Process
Improvement Method**

This simple method is based on our research of how to meet employees' time pressures and provide an uncomplicated way to get people managing and improving processes. Meets the Stage 2 requirement for a tool to move people from cost reduction to process management. Simple and effective, the method is quick, easy-to-understand and brings results.

**Chapter 12 -
Service
Improvement**

Even Stage 2 companies find service delivery challenging. The chapter explains how customers think and what your organization can do to improve service performance. Included is an effective tool to clear up service delivery issues.

**Chapter 13 -
Facilitating
Improvement**

Stage 2 companies work at the management side of improvement. Facilitating improvement discussions is crucial to your company's progress. Covers the practical keys to becoming an effective facilitator. Listening, asking questions and handling individuals are explained along with tips for effective meetings.

**Chapter 14 -
Coaching**

A number of practical suggestions on developing your coaching ability. Use the included test and see if you are making progress in your coaching efforts.

Chapter Fit To The
SMG Improvement Method

The following illustration shows how the tool collection equips a manager to effectively implement the SMG Improvement Method.

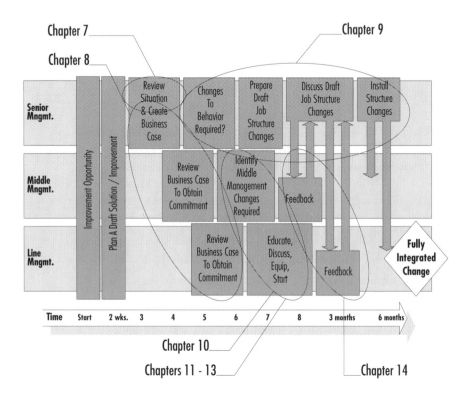

7

A Simple, Strategic Business Review

Linking Strategy and Activities

A PERIODIC REVIEW OF YOUR ORGANIZATION'S BUSINESS SITUATION is critical. Changes happen so quickly today it is dangerous to go a year without reexamining the fit between the business situation, resources and strategy.

In many organizations, the review process is formalized, overcomplicated and lacking in relevance. Managers react in a predictable fashion. They delay it as long as possible or do the bare minimum to get through the process unscathed. When finished, the resulting document is distributed and often filed unopened until the start of next year's review process. The managers complain the process has little bearing on their ongoing activities. This is ironic since the objective of planning is to shape activities. We find a simpler planning model with less overhead is the answer.

This analysis format is not meant to replace multimillion dollar studies performed by planning specialists. It is designed to give senior managers the ability to quickly gauge current activities to see if they are supporting strategic objectives. This is a key Stage 2 requirement.

A simple, quick and effective review allows managers to regularly check their business environment for potential opportunities and potential trouble. Businesses can become preoccupied with current activities and lose sight of strategic activities. A regular review identifies recent changes that may affect plans and activities. As a result, management can recognize issues, prevent potential problems, and react to ensure continued success. The results of the review are packaged into a business case and presented to the employees as the improvement justification.

This review represents the first or internal motivation step in the motivation sandwich model *(Chp. 5)*. The three steps include: presenting the business reasons for the change to the employees; providing understanding and skills training; and modifying jobs to create ongoing motivation to continue the activities.

Why do you need to perform this review and present it to the employees? Don't employees understand why management makes specific decisions? The short answer is no. Some may ask why you don't merely print up the strategic objectives on a brochure and give a copy to every person in the company? It would be a quick way of getting the message out. Quick, but not effective.

The trouble is, that clarity or understanding is relative. What we believe is crystal clear can be quite confusing to a group of people with different perceptions and experiences. My colleague Bruce Fournier tells the following story to illustrate how information can be perceived differently.

Earlier in his career, Bruce was an air force tactical aircraft commander, leading submarine-finding flights over the north Atlantic. When his crew returned to base after one winter flight, they found the landing strip invisible, obscured by clouds, snow, and winter weather. They carefully descended, talking constantly with the control tower operator. Finally breaking through the clouds, they found they weren't aligned with the center of the runway. They were looking at snow rather than asphalt. The pilot opened the throttles and went up to try again. The second descent was more successful: they were now in correct alignment with the runway, but as they broke through the cloud cover, directly in front of them was a large snowplow laboring to remove the snow from the runway. The engines roared again as the pilot aborted the landing, barely missing the snowplow. The exhausted (and exasperated) crew hoped the next pass would be both more successful and less eventful. While descending this time, there was some pointed conversation with the tower. After successfully landing the plane on the third attempt, the crew went to discuss the snowplow problem with the tower controller. In his defense, the controller said: "I don't know what happened; I told the snowplow operator to *clear* the runway."

To a pilot, *clearing* a runway means to get off the runway as quickly as possible. To a snowplow operator, *clearing* a runway means removing the snow. The difference in perspective nearly cost a number of people their lives that day.

We want to give employees an opportunity to clearly understand our business and why suggested changes or improvements are needed. The intent is to package the strategic issues, present the business situation to employees, encourage personal commitment to the objectives, and provide a guide to help them prioritize their own improvement activities.

It usually takes a day to go through the analysis the first time. Don't try to labor over each section, but divide up the time and cover the key issues. Repeat reviews take much less time because you only look at changes from the previous review. Management can use periodic reviews to reexamine the assumptions and structure of the organization.

These review headings are based on and adapted from the first few chapters of *Strategic Management* by Mark C. Baetz and Paul W. Beamish. This is an excellent text covering the topic with a refreshing economy of words.

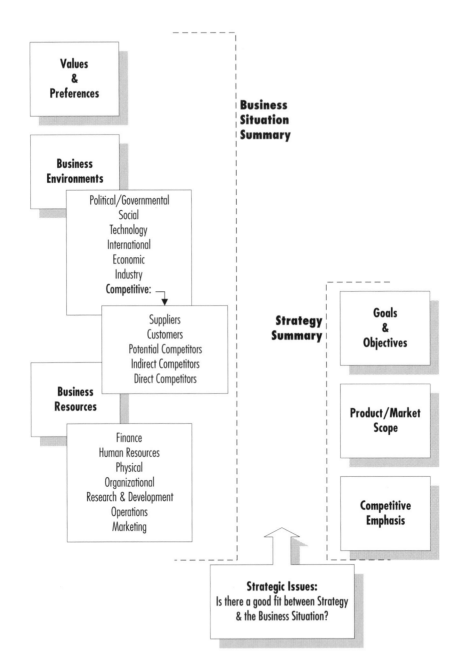

Values
&
Preferences

Business
Situation
Summary

Business
Environments

Political/Governmental
Social
Technology
International
Economic
Industry
Competitive:

Strategy
Summary

Goals
&
Objectives

Suppliers
Customers
Potential Competitors
Indirect Competitors
Direct Competitors

Business
Resources

Product/Market
Scope

Finance
Human Resources
Physical
Organizational
Research & Development
Operations
Marketing

Competitive
Emphasis

Strategic Issues:
Is there a good fit between Strategy
& the Business Situation?

The review covers four categories:

1. Values and Preferences
2. Business Environments
3. Corporate Resources
4. Strategy

1. Values and Preferences

Describe what is important to your organization. Are people, customers, profits or technology important? What choices does the organization make on a continual basis? List the things you would tell someone who asks you what it's like to work in your organization. Summarize the way the company treats people. Describe the way it functions. Is it traditional, nontraditional, bureaucratic or open, etc? Be honest. You aren't discussing anything here your employees don't already know.

2. Business Environments

In the following business environments, describe anything that may affect your business situation and future plans.

POLITICAL/GOVERNMENTAL

List any political and government issues that currently affect or will affect your customers, suppliers, employees, funding, or relevant regulations you now work with. Include any environmental or developmental concerns.

SOCIAL

Are there changes in your customers' or employees' demographics. Are consumption, earning or usage patterns changing? Is there a shifting of factors by geographic region? Are there changing habits or trends among your end users that are due to social changes?

TECHNOLOGICAL

Is your industry technology driven? Does it look at new materials, new techniques, new equipment, computerization? What in the technological area is affecting your decision-making as you look at the future?

INTERNATIONAL

Are there going to be changes in demand or changes in your distribution channels? Are you exporting or considering exporting? What are the trade realities of setting up a new operation or maintaining an existing one? What are some of the international pressures that could affect your product and service choices?

ECONOMIC

Are there interest rate or funding issues? Are there economic pressures on your customers? Does it look like there will be changes in disposable income for your customers? Will your situation allow normal borrowing or is there added risk that could require a higher rate of interest?

INDUSTRY

Discuss your marketplace briefly. Why do people come to you for your products or services? Is it a mature or young, growing market? How many markets do you participate in? Are there seasonal demand patterns or other issues associated with your specific industry?

COMPETITIVE

Your company's competitive situation is made up of a number of components which depend on your industry. Examine your competitive situation using the following guide and create a report card-style rating.

The five competitive components are:

Suppliers The organization may buy from *suppliers*. Professional service organizations often don't have many suppliers.

Customers You sell to *customers*.

Potential Competitors Organizations that could come into your marketplace—is your industry inviting to them?

Indirect Competitors   Organizations selling products or services that could replace or substitute for the products or services your company provides.

Direct Competitors   Organizations that offer the same products and services in your marketplace.

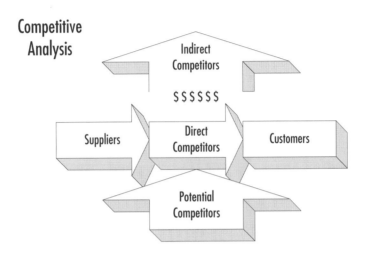

SUPPLIERS

Evaluate your organization's relationship with its suppliers. The evaluation should focus on how suppliers affect the gainful operation of your company. The report card rating can go from *excellent*, to *satisfactory*, to *requires corrective action*.

- Relative size: Is your organization a big player in your marketplace; are your suppliers smaller companies with little leverage over you? Or, is the situation reversed: are you small and your suppliers large organizations? The degree of leverage affects your costs and flexibility. If your suppliers are large companies, could they purchase a competitor and begin to compete directly with you?

- Are the supplied products and services available from a large number of vendors or just a few (limits flexibility and leverage)?

- Are the supplied products and services proprietary or a key part of your company's marketing formula? Would switching to another vendor's products be costly or difficult? Both limit flexibility and reduce your company's leverage over your suppliers.

CUSTOMERS

Evaluate your organization's relationship with its customers. The evaluation should focus on how customers affect the gainful operation of your company. The report card rating can go from *excellent*, to *satisfactory*, to *requires corrective action*.

- Relative size: Is your organization a big player in your marketplace; are your customers smaller companies with little leverage over you? Or is the situation reversed with you being small and your customers large organizations? The degree of leverage affects your margins and flexibility. If your customers are large companies, could they purchase a competitor and begin to compete directly with you?

- Are the products and services you provide purchased by a large number of customers or just a few (limits flexibility, profit margins, and the leverage your company receives from its development efforts)?

- Are the supplied products and services you provide proprietary or a key part of your customer's marketing formula or product design? Would switching to another vendor be costly or difficult for your customer? Both affect flexibility and enhance your company's leverage over your customers.

POTENTIAL COMPETITORS

If your industry is growing and profitable, it will attract organizations with related skills. They will enter your marketplace and become direct competitors. The evaluation concerns how attractive your industry is and whether barriers exist to keep them out. This affects the long-term gainful operation of your company. The report card rating can go from *attractive* (potential risk), to *average*, to *unattractive* (low risk).

- Markets grow through stages from *growing* (profitable), to *shedding* (less profitable with many competitors merging or going out of business), to *stable* (low profits and steady number of competitors), to *declining* (still lower profits and reductions in the number of competitors). If your industry is growing and profitable, other companies will consider participating; this can reduce your sales and/or margins.

- Are there unique issues that make it difficult for potential competitors? For example, the large number of coupons, the large marketing expenditures, and shelf placement charges make it difficult for new breakfast-cereal companies to enter that marketplace.

- Does your organization have a unique identity that may be difficult to duplicate?

- Does your industry require significant capital costs to start or continue operating (e.g., setting up a nationwide air carrier or cellular network)?

- Is there a strong reaction by you and your fellow competitors to a new competitor in your marketplace (e.g., retail reaction to big box stores)? Who can best survive the financial impact of the competitive reaction?

INDIRECT COMPETITORS

An important and frequently neglected area. Indirect competitors offer similar (not identical) products or services that can vacuum dollars from your industry. This affects the long-term gainful operation of your company. The report card rating can go from *low* (little ability to draw away sales), to *average*, to *high* (able to draw away sales).

- Are there other products or services that can be substituted at a lower price (e.g., a ski operation sells recreation services not just skiing; recreation dollars can be spent in a number of ways, as in a trip to a Caribbean island)?

- Is it difficult for your customers to switch to an alternative? If consumers make a significant investment in ski equipment, they are more likely to purchase skiing services than ocean cruises. The investment serves to raise switching costs. A restaurant selling Chinese food also competes with pizza outlets for takeout dollars, but customers can easily switch menus. The same principle applies to industry.

- Are technological advances merging previously distinct industries? (e.g., high speed network printers competing with traditional photocopier applications)?

DIRECT COMPETITORS

The number, relative competence, and animosity of your direct competitors affect the short-term and long-term gainful operation of your company. The report card rating can go from *damaging* (many organizations in concentrated, fierce competition), to *taxing* (direct but bearable), to *livable* (not a major problem), to *light* (competitors don't significantly affect your margins).

- Look at your industry's growth stage (see potential competitors); growing industries have an increasing number of dollars to share among competitors. Industries that are shedding competitors experience fierce competition for available dollars.

- How distinctive are your company's offerings. Are they easy or hard to duplicate? Does extensive marketing activity support your offerings and make direct competition more difficult?

- Are there boundaries or barriers that limit competition (e.g., long-distance transportation costs for a printing company)?

- Are there many or few direct competitors?

- Are competitors adding information or service components that are difficult to duplicate (e.g., a computerized tracking system for a courier company)?

To summarize the competitive analysis, take all five areas into account and evaluate your marketplace. Is it a difficult or easy place to earn a reasonable return on an investment?

Indicate which of the five competitive components make it easier or harder to survive and prosper. List the supporting reasons for your judgment and any actions that should be taken to improve your business situation.

3. Corporate Resources

These represent the resources the company can apply to the strategy. Your organization's resources *should* match your needs as identified in your strategy and competitive/industry analysis. The key word is *should*.

FINANCE

What are the financial resources of the organization? What are the strengths and weaknesses of the financial position of the company? Are funds available from a parent company? Does the parent company restrict financial/ spending options? Are financial controls tight or loose within your company?

HUMAN RESOURCES

What are the strengths and weaknesses in your human resources situation? Describe the management team in terms of leadership and effectiveness. Describe the workforce. Are they teachable, flexible, educated, enthusiastic? Are people open to change? Are there individuals who are particularly gifted? Describe management's relationship with the workforce? Is management dictatorial or bureaucratic? Does the human resources situation give you a strategic advantage? Why?

PHYSICAL RESOURCES

Are there advantages or weaknesses to your physical facilities? Rented facilities are an advantage to an organization that values flexibility. Are the facilities new or older? Will renovation costs be required to allow the organization to properly service its customers? Is there enough space? Is communication affected because the workforce is spread over a number of offices?

ORGANIZATIONAL

As an organization, what do you own? Are there patents? Do you own a unique process or have a particular brand position in the marketplace? Do people look to your product or service as the benchmark by which others are measured? Is your product or service formula difficult to duplicate? Do you have a flat organizational structure that facilitates the flow of communication? How capable and relevant are the supporting systems (information, accounting, quality, training, and management development)?

RESEARCH AND DEVELOPMENT

What are the strengths and weaknesses of your R&D effort? Are you developing new products and services based on customer demand, market research, or untested, management intuition? Are new products and services ready to be implemented the moment the development department releases them or are long periods required to adapt them to organizational and marketplace realities? Is the present and planned effort sufficient for continued success?

OPERATIONS

What are the strengths and weaknesses of the unit's operations? Are you consistently able to meet customers' expectations? Are you overselling in sales or under-performing in operations? Do you have delivery problems on products and services? Do you have inconsistencies throughout the operation? Do customers get consistent service day-after-day, year-after-year?

MARKETING

What are the strengths and weaknesses of the marketing effort of the organization? Is marketing passing back clear, quality information to the rest of the organization about what customers need and expect? Does the organization understand customers' needs after marketing explains what they are? Do you take the extra time to identify market segments that will be profitable before developing new products for those segments? Basically, marketing should be more than the selling arm of the organization. Marketing is the organization's eyes and ears, helping to look for places to put products and services to maintain growth and profitability.

4. Strategy

Strategy is a combination of three elements. The *Goals and Objectives* describe the direction and measurable issues related to achieving goals. The *Product and Marketing Offering* describes the products or services that are or will be offered by the organization to its customers. The company achieves its goals and objectives by providing the listed products and services to the marketplace. The *Competitive Emphasis* describes your marketplace characteristics or the reasons customers consume your products and services rather than those of a competitor.

GOALS AND OBJECTIVES

List the organization's goals and objectives including any sales, profit, performance, customer satisfaction, or related expectation. List objectives for company growth, management development, market or product development.

PRODUCT/MARKET OFFERING

Are you looking to increase sales to existing markets or to develop new markets? Are you looking to develop new products and take them to existing markets or to go into new markets with new products? Discuss the products and services that will help you reach your goals and objectives? Which specific products and services are going to be the key work horses that will carry your organization to where it should be?

COMPETITIVE EMPHASIS

What is distinctive about your company's offerings that make customers seek them out? Why does your company exist? Why don't customers go somewhere else? What are the advantages that your products or services have compared to those of your competition?

Summarize

You have looked at four categories with a number of elements under each. Take the information gathered and put it on one page. This will force you to choose only the important issues. Summarize the collected information until you have approximately four points or less under each element.

Are There Gaps?

Discuss the summary of the Values and Preferences, Environments, Resources and Strategy categories. Evaluate whether there is a lack of fit among the areas. Compare each area with other areas. Will your corporate resources allow your company to achieve its goals and objectives? What could stop you from accomplishing your objectives?

As you discuss these issues, you will identify key activities or required changes that will be the success factors your organization must address during the next one or two years.

The review process can be quite beneficial. During a review, one client realized they had few competitors in their unique field. They started holding prices when customers asked about reductions. They also introduced new products at higher prices than previously thought possible.

Another organization saw that competition was putting downward pressure on prices; costs were rising; and shareholder expectations were escalating. This meant internal cost reductions and performance improvements had to be the focus for the short-term. Time was taken to present this information to all employees. Groups immediately started to reduce costs while streamlining the operation. Later when a few smaller offices were closed and some people were laid off, employee morale didn't take a nose dive. Employees understood the business realities and knew a changing business situation, rather than management greed, caused the changes.

In the next chapter, we discuss how to present the review findings to the employees to help them better understand the business and the need for the planned improvement.

8 | Creating The Business Case

Building Employee Commitment Through Internal Motivation

EFFECTIVE COMMUNICATION OF YOUR BUSINESS SITUATION is a key Stage 2 skill. Employees and managers must understand what the organization is about to do, and why those actions are important.

This is not a business case in the business school sense of the term. The term "business case" used in this book denotes a presentation that justifies the planned improvement. This includes the issues uncovered during the Strategic Review *(Chp. 7)*.

In *The Art of War*, Sun Tzu said: "Those whose upper and lower ranks have the same desire will be victorious;" and "A common aim or goal is required to unify the people." If the organization's strategy can be communicated simply and clearly, people can use it to guide activity choices.

The characteristics of a good business case presentation are listed with practical suggestions for the presentation format. An effective business case presentation should be clear, concise, and free of both jargon and propaganda.

Clear

By clear, we mean pretested. After recording the essentials you want to communicate, go through the material a number of times, take out unnecessary information, and clarify the remaining material. When putting together a presentation, it is sometimes difficult to predict how the material will be received. Consider your audience and run through your material with the supervisors and middle managers. Ask them whether it is boring, unrealistic, or complicated. Revise the presentation, then ask for comments from a sample group of employees. At the end of the presentation, ask them to restate the main points. If they cannot easily restate the few specific issues and outline your suggested improvements, then go back and make it even more understandable.

Concise

The entire presentation should take a maximum of one hour. Forty-five minutes is optimum. Adults have short attention spans. Keep the material short; hit the high points; and focus on the improvement as a logical reaction to the business situation.

Jargon-Free

Use words everyone understands. This seems to be difficult for some managers. If you use jargon in day-to-day communication, then it can be difficult to detect. If your spouse can't understand the presentation, then you can be sure that a large number of employees won't either. Put aside the buzzwords and your organization's three-letter acronyms. Explain things in simple terms.

For example, use *model* or *perspective* rather than the widely misunderstood *paradigm*. For *deploy*, use *install, position* or *distribute*. The key is to make the language so straightforward that even newcomers get the right message. As mentioned earlier *(Chp. 3)*, jargon divides the company into those who know and those who are too self-conscious to stop you and ask. Build bridges—not barriers.

Propaganda-Free

It is important that the presentation realistically present the company, warts and all. It should not be a psychological exercise. It should reflect the awareness that employees already know what is going on. They have been waiting for someone to be honest enough to discuss the situation freely. The presentation should also not be a forum to advance a particular point of view. Objectivity and sincerity are the keys.

Every company is a collection of strengths and weaknesses. The presentation should touch on both, but don't focus on the negative. If the company has been stuffy and bureaucratic, but steps are being taken to improve participation and responsiveness, tell them about the changes. If management cannot discuss the situation without getting defensive, find someone the employees respect to deliver the message (let's hope that's you). Most employees don't expect managers to be perfect. They do expect managers to be able to admit mistakes. Keep the presentation realistic and objective.

Suggested Format For Business Case Presentation

Outline:

- What We Are Striving To Become
- What We Are Now
- Changes In Our Business Environments
- Our Resources
- Our Goals
- Implications - Gaps
- What We Need To Do To Close The Gaps

WHAT WE ARE STRIVING TO BECOME

Summarize the type of organization you want to become over the next few years:

- More people participate in decisions before they are made.
- There is less distance between management and employees.
- There is greater respect for people.
- We anticipate and plan for possible situations.

WHAT WE ARE NOW

Describe how people may have characterized your organization in the past and how they see it now:

- Traditional?
- Bureaucratic?
- Stuffy?
- Undisciplined?
- Reactive? Fun? Respected?

CHANGES IN OUR BUSINESS ENVIRONMENTS

List the changes or trends in the business environments that will affect your organization. Discuss one or two points for each applicable business environment. The environments are: Industry; Political/ Governmental; Social; Technological; International; Economic; and Competitive.

Hint: Cover the industry first, explaining some of the background or basics of operating in your industry for new employees or employees who are involved in only a limited area of the organization. This will help them appreciate the issues raised later in the presentation.

Describe a change or trend, then clearly describe the major implication for your company. This part of the presentation is a series of changes or trends, each accompanied by the potential impact of the issue on your business.

OUR RESOURCES

List the resources available to your organization. The resource categories are: Financial; People (including management); Organizational; Operations; and Research & Development.

Hint: Try to strike a balance between optimism and realism. Everything said should be perceived as balanced, realistic and reasonable. If there are weaknesses or areas needing improvement, it is important and appropriate to mention them here. However, the way you mention them is even more important. Don't assign blame to a less-adequate group. When discussing weaker areas, emphasize that outside factors or changing requirements can cause some activities to appear less important. The appropriate response is to periodically examine all major processes.

Don't allow this reflection to become an opportunity to trash management. **The objective is to build respect for management, not destroy it.** By presenting the business and what's happening in the business environment, you will build respect as employees come to appreciate the reasons behind management's current decisions.

BUSINESS GOALS

Describe specific goals and objectives; touch on categories of products or services that will be important; and simply explain why customers come to you rather than your competitors. Cover all three components.

Hint: Try to be candid in describing where you want to go and the products and services that will support the direction. If there is a balance to be struck between candor and confidentiality, err on the side of candor. Why? It shows employees that you trust them more than you fear a leak to a competitor. By sharing plans in general terms, you are more likely to gain employee support (especially if the reasoning is sound and understandable).

We don't recommend that you put the presentation in writing. It is important for the employees to hear and see the material, but a written report might fall into outsiders' hands. In our experience to date, no employee has asked for a written copy of the presentation.

IMPLICATIONS - GAPS

Consider the fit between the company's Values and Preferences, Situation, Resources and Strategy. Describe the missing parts of the picture. Describe the opportunities that best apply to your company's combination of situation and strengths.

Hint: The list shouldn't include 50 items. It should highlight the few major issues from your analysis.

WHAT WE NEED TO DO TO CLOSE THE GAPS

Describe the specific issues as well as the types of activities and behavior that will allow your company to exploit these opportunities and minimize problems. The points may look similar to these:

• Improve cooperation between groups A & B. The improved cooperation must look like this . . . . in order for these projects to succeed.

- Prices will be forced down to X, so we need to reduce our prices by Y.
- We must train our people to simply document, improve, and manage the processes they are involved in. This training will begin in the next three months.
- Product/Service development must focus on profitable markets such as . . . . .
- Productivity must increase to . . . . . to help ensure continued contracts with sufficient margins.

CLOSING

At the end of the presentation, ask for the personal support of the employees to help the organization and each other make the necessary changes to survive and continue. Let them ask questions and make comments.

9

The Reinforcing Structure™

Structuring For Lasting Change

IF YOU WANT TO MOVE TO THE ACTIVITY FOCUS OF STAGE 2, this chapter is vital. The Reinforcing Structure™ described here outlines four types of job structures or levers organizations can use to influence behavior. These structures provide the *external motivation* described earlier in the motivation sandwich behavior model *(Chp. 5)*. The four types of job structures provide the ongoing motivation your organization needs to sustain important activities.

We have seen successful organizations employ mechanisms or levers that encourage people to continue to perform key tasks. Our research uncovered the four types and they are presented with examples to help you put them to use.

Typically, managers communicate the reason an improvement or change is required, train the individuals in the new way of doing things, and hope for the best. They don't intentionally install anything to reinforce the new behavior. As a result, the long-term survival of the improvement is left to chance. As other urgent issues arise, attention is drawn away to other areas and the initiative fades away.

Successful companies: Stage 2 companies find that even one well designed structure can shape behavior for many employees.

Blue Mountain Resorts Limited is a wonderful winter/summer resort complex located about an hour north of Toronto. Blue Mountain gives every guest a card. The card asks guests whether Blue Mountain met, fell below or exceeded their expectations (when compared with other resorts of its type). The organization has tracked the responses over the last number of years and has noted that customers are more pleased with the resort each year. This one satisfaction measure creates constant pressure within the organization to look at customer issues and deal with them quickly and correctly. Staff—from ski rental and slide ride operators to golf pros, cleaners and desk people—all feel the same pressure to delight and exceed the expectations of customers. By tracking and publishing this one measure, the organization has successfully created a culture that seeks to constantly improve its service delivery.

In one SMG research project, we asked companies to indicate whether they had made changes to any of the four elements to support their new improvement efforts. The results showed a marked difference between organizations. The organizations showed greater progress as they made changes in two or more of the elements of the Reinforcing Structure™. As organizations employed more structural elements to encourage key behavior, improvement progress became more predictable and progress increased.

Jack Smith, the CEO of General Motors, discovered the power of structure as he plowed through GM's bulk. The problems of size, inertia and resistance were significant at General Motors. As Jack lead the renovation, he found the problem was not the workers; the main problem was (job) structure. *"The problem was never the people,"* he said. *"It was the screwed-up structure. We had to change it."* Mechanisms and measurements within the organization didn't motivate employees to behave properly (e.g., cooperate, problem-solve, innovate). Some of the structures within GM worked against proposed improvements. Jack Smith understood that GM's structure was driving behavior, *individual behavior*, in the wrong direction. GM didn't have a people problem; the fault was the structure hidden below the surface of the organization. Using structure to encourage behavior is the focus of this chapter.

What are the four elements of the Reinforcing Structure™?

1. **Organizational Structure**
2. **Performance Measures**
3. **Employee Evaluation Criteria**
4. **Rewards And Incentives**

1. Organizational Structure

The first element is the organizational reporting structure. It is the way the organization determines how different departments, groups and teams interact with the balance of the organization. There are two sides to the Organizational Structure element. The first question is whether the goals and objectives of the organization are reflected in the reporting structure; the second is whether functional departments impede or enhance the work at hand.

First let's look at the goals and objectives. A company's mission statement proclaims human resources development as a key to its survival. The company has the Human Resources Department report directly to the president. This shows that the company has entrenched its mission into its reporting structure, giving sufficient power to the position to accomplish its objectives. Compare this with a similar company whose mission statement also embraces human resources development as a key activity. The Human Resources Department in this company reports through the Finance Department. Individuals understand that human resources is as important as any other finance function such as Accounts Receivable or Accounts Payable. By viewing the reporting structure, employees know how important an area is (or isn't).

Now let's consider whether functional departments impede or enhance work activities. Many companies design their organization around job functions. Often the functional departments don't cooperate because each has a different set of priorities. Occasionally key processes or projects lack resources due to conflicting interests. Problems arise when needed resources reside in groups that are not directly involved in the process or project. Because the resources report through different managers, the conflicting priorities create frustration and delay.

Your Organizational Structure can better encourage activities if your goals are reflected in your reporting structure and major processes are not hindered by functional interests.

EXAMPLE:

A technical group and an operations group have an adversarial relationship. The organizational structure looks like this:

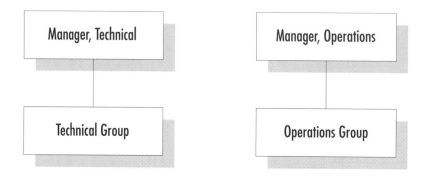

Different Objectives = Different Priorities

Often the managers are evaluated on departmental outcomes rather than the performance of the organization as a whole. The technical manager could be motivated by budget measures. To ensure budget dollars are spent wisely, all requests for help are pooled, then evaluated so only the best projects receive resources. As a result, new requests for technical assistance are not immediately considered.

The operations manager sees the technical group as nonresponsive and unable to see the bigger picture. The underlying problem is managers who have different objectives and priorities. Their priorities affect their activity choices.

The problem can be solved in two ways.

One: The operations manager could be made responsible for both groups. This would resolve the problem of conflicting objectives. Each group would have similar priorities and cooperation would improve. The principle involves giving managers control over the resources required to accomplish a task.

This could also cause a problem if the manager objects to reporting to an old peer. We will assume the decision can be justified for the sake of the organization and the potential benefits from cooperation far outweigh the bruised ego.

The structure now looks like this:

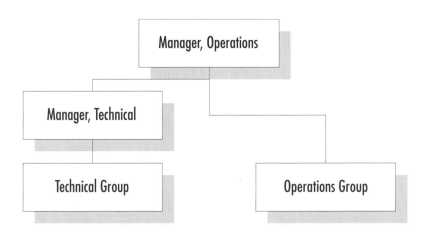

Unified Objectives = Similar Priorities + Cooperation

Two: The performance measures or evaluation criteria for the managers could be changed to gauge their departments' contribution to the organization's objectives. These structures are described in the next sections.

Are there two groups within your organization that have difficulty cooperating? What are the reasons for the lack of performance? Could both groups be merged? Could management be evaluated differently to encourage cooperation?

2. Performance Measures

David Vossbrink, Public Relations Manager for the city of Sunnyvale, California, states: "To motivate correct employee behavior, the most important thing we can do is to pick the right performance measure." Sunnyvale's ability to select the *right* performance measure is one of the main reasons why it was voted the best place to start a business in the United States. Vossbrink says the measures you employ to evaluate an area's performance powerfully affect the behavior of the individuals within the area. Depend

-ing on the measure selected, the resulting behavior can benefit or impede the organization's pursuit of its goals.

Performance measures are the most important job structure. They are inexpensive, effective and can be created quickly. Two things should be considered when deciding on a set of measures.

One: A balance of behavior is often required; using two measures on the same group can motivate activities that represent a compromise between different objectives. For example, a department store could reduce costs by reducing the number of clerks in the store, but this would have a negative effect on customer satisfaction. By evaluating store managers, using a proper weighting of both customer satisfaction and cost control, a store chain can obtain balanced actions.

Two: Define the goal you want to achieve—then select measures that will accomplish the goal.

GOAL: ENCOURAGE COOPERATION

A performance measure that deals with how well the entire business unit performs is useful for creating cooperative pressure. The principle here is to measure departments within the unit on the performance of the entire unit. The departments then have similar priorities; this encourages cooperation. Example: Measure all departments on how profitable the unit is or on the customer satisfaction rating for the entire unit.

GOAL: ENCOURAGE IMPROVEMENT

A performance measure that compares current performance with past performance is useful in encouraging improvement behavior over time.

An effective performance measure is not distorted by changes in the workplace. Measure a department's output (e.g., billings, units produced, or customers served), but calculate the output per employee. This keeps the measure useful and relevant, even when comparing periods with different staffing levels.

Example: A productivity measure could record the number of transactions completed per *payroll* hour. This measure remains useful whether the number of individuals working in the area goes up or down. It is also not affected by overtime pay because the calculation uses payroll hours not payroll dollars (each overtime hour would still be one payroll hour).

GOAL: ENCOURAGE CONSISTENCY

The checklist is a performance measure that is effective in encouraging consistent behavior. A checklist can ensure a person completes the entire set of activities related to a particular process step. It can be used to encourage consistency among employees or in situations where employees lack the required discipline to finish an entire list of tasks (e.g., sales?). Identify the important elements involved in completing a particular step and record them. The list can be used to check off each element when completed. The beauty of a well-designed checklist is that it enforces consistent behavior without requiring a great deal of supervisory time.

When I recently purchased a mini-van, the salesman told me that I should allow 45 minutes to pick up the keys. When I expressed surprise, he explained there were a number of things about the car I needed to know. During the session, he went through a list that greatly increased my appreciation for the dealership, the car, and the service department. At the conclusion, he asked me to sign the bottom of the checklist form, confirming that I had discussed the listed issues and understood them.

In this situation, the checklist creates knowledgeable customers. Knowledgeable customers are better able to appreciate the value provided by the dealership. Sales people could be tempted to rush through the presentation and finish the transaction as quickly as possible, but the salesman mentioned the sale would not be credited to his quota until the signed checklist arrived with the payment. This created a real desire to complete the presentation.

Very little management time is required to ensure the presentations continue. The performance measure (the checklist) was also matched with an incentive (the crediting of the car to his quota for the year). Both combine to create positive employee behavior.

3. Employee Evaluation Criteria

Most companies do not have an effective employee evaluation process. Often, the evaluation discussion is narrowly focused on the department's or individual's activities. Little is done to create positive motivation for employees. Organizations are missing an opportunity to impress on their employees the behavior that is expected.

An organization can highlight for the employee exactly the behavior that is expected and required for the organization's success. By focusing on the required behavior, companies avoid rudderless conversations about attitude (which is virtually impossible to pin down).

What are the behaviors that organizations need to succeed? Ralph Stayer, CEO, Johnsonville Foods, Inc., of Sheboygan, Wisconsin, reveals some of the behaviors his company looks for in their evaluation system in his article, "How I Learned To Let My Workers Lead" (Harvard Business Review, Nov.-Dec. 1990 - Reprint #90610).

- Customer Satisfaction
- Cost-Effectiveness
- Responsibility
- Ideas
- Problem Solver/ Problem Preventer
- Safety
- Quality Image
- Contribution To Groups
- Communication
- Willingness To Work Together
- Attendance and Timeliness
- Lifelong Learning

How can an organization reinforce key behaviors? Here is an effective method for ensuring your evaluation program encourages positive behavior.

BEHAVIOR-ANCHORED RATING SCALE

A behavior-anchored rating scale shows different types of behavior and asks employees to indicate the box that best represents their behavior in that category. This technique has several advantages over more traditional methods.

First, it doesn't use a numerical ranking. Numerical ratings usually don't have clearly described criteria. As a result, the judgment appears arbitrary and open to distortion or favoritism.

Second, the behaviors targeted can be broad and positive for the entire organization rather than focused on the individual's objectives. The behavior-anchored ranking scale covers more general criteria, while a list of the individual's performance objectives covers only specific expectations. The combination is powerful and it provides a balance between behavior and accountability.

Third, this technique describes in concrete terms the behavior the organization values.

Some examples are given on the next few pages. The behaviors being evaluated are problem solving, teamwork and customer satisfaction. Please read the examples to see the logic behind the descriptions.

PROBLEM SOLVING

(adapted from Ralph Stayer's article)

Do I contribute to solving or preventing problems? Do I anticipate problem situations? Do I keep lines of communication open with my supervisor and other members of my process team?

( )	( )	( )	( )
Has difficulty in recognizing & acting on problems. Doesn't actively participate in problem solving activities. Doesn't pass on problem information to prevent reoccurrence.	Occasionally recognizes problem situations. Takes preventive action in some cases. Sometimes participates in problem solving discussions. Occasionally passes on information to prevent reoccurrence.	Often sees problem situations before they arise and in most cases takes preventive measures. Generally participates in trying to solve problems and prevent reoccurrence. Reliably passes on information to others to prevent reoccurrence.	Looks ahead to see problems before they arise and takes action to prevent their occurrence. Enthusiastically participates in problem solving discussions, helping others to look ahead to prevent similar occurrences. Always communicates to help others to avoid problems.

TEAMWORK

Do I share responsibility and assist others in achieving my team's goals?

( )	( )	( )	( )
Attends team sessions, but doesn't contribute or share experience with others. Doesn't participate in team activities, but is willing to criticize group efforts. Shows little interest in helping the team achieve its goals. Frequently lets personal interests create disagreements. Unwilling to share experience with others.	Attends team sessions and occasionally shares with the group. Participates in team activities when specifically asked to, but without extra effort. Occasionally shares experience with others when specifically asked.	Attends team sessions and contributes regularly to the discussion. Participates willingly in team activities and completes assigned tasks. Shows interest in helping the team achieve its goals. Willing to share experience with others when asked.	Helps to coordinate and attends team sessions. Strongly contributes to the discussion. Participates willingly in team activities, completes assigned tasks and helps ensure that others complete their assignments. Shows personal interest in setting goals and helping the team achieve them. Always willing to share specific information to help others improve.

CUSTOMER SATISFACTION

Am I concerned with satisfying the company's customers? Am I concerned with satisfying the requirements of those inside my organization who receive work from me? Am I looking for ways to improve my work so it is easier for my customers to use? Do I take appropriate and immediate action to correct problems and ensure customer satisfaction?

( )	( )	( )	( )
Problems that affect the company's customers are not given much concern. There is little or no effort to ensure that internal customers can effectively use what is produced. Corrective action must be suggested by others and others must follow up to ensure completion.	Occasionally considers the impact of work activities on company's customers. Internal customers are considered when others point out opportunities for improvement. Corrective action is completed when required but requires occasional supervision.	Generally considers the impact of work activities on the company's customers. Periodically reviews own work to ensure that work produced can be easily used by internal customers. Corrective action is thought of, but action is not taken until approved by someone else.	Always considers the impact on external customers. Considers own work and revises it to better meet internal customers' needs. Takes personal responsibility for problems and immediately looks for ways to correct errors and improve performance. Action is taken immediately (supervisors told later) with no follow-up required.

IMPLEMENTATION

Employees indicate the boxes that best represent their behavior in the last year (or six months). Supervisors then indicate their assessment (after discussions with other supervisors) of the employees' behavior. The evaluation discussion then centers around the gaps between the two assessments.

Follow this format to create your own behavior-anchored rating scales.

1. **Identify Key Criteria.** Examine the job to determine the criteria you want to encourage.

2. **Collect Examples Of Behavior.** Ask employees and supervisors for descriptions of problem solving (or any other criteria) behavior within the target job.

3. **Assign To Position On Scale.** Build the scale so that normal, positive behavior is positioned just above the midpoint on the scale. Research shows that most people think they are at least average or slightly above. Building the scale in this way avoids resistance (or damage to self-esteem). It also lets you get on with the job at hand—evaluating behavior and clearly communicating behavioral expectations.

4. **Adjust The Degree Of The Behavior To Fill In The Scale.** If the positive behavior is above the midpoint, imagine more positive behavior and fill in the high side. The next box down from normal should equate to behavior that needs improvement. The lowest box should reflect behavior that needs serious work.

5. **Develop Draft Appraisal Form.** Combine the scales with some job-specific objectives and show this tool to the individuals involved. Give it out so they can read it, then meet to go over the elements one by one.

6. **Obtain Employee Comments.** Give them some more time to make some comments to you in private; some will be reluctant to voice opinions in a group.

7. **Train Supervisors.** Role play the evaluation discussion with the supervisors. When a disagreement arises over rating gaps (usually when an employee rating is higher than the supervisor's—the other direction doesn't seem to cause the same problem), have the supervisor ask for examples in the last year where the employee demonstrated the behavior in question. Let the employee think of instances without interruption from the supervisor. Studies show

people cannot fabricate a story quickly enough to lie through this evaluation discussion. The result is a description that might cause the supervisor to modify the ranking. In the absence of a description, the original ranking remains.

4. Rewards & Incentives

Companies immediately think of rewards and incentives, the most complex element in the Reinforcing Structure™, when they want to influence employee behavior. As a result, organizations commit to programs (gainsharing, profit-sharing, bonuses, etc.) without first considering the behavioral impact. Behavior *is* created, but it frequently causes additional problems. For example, bonuses for individual departments (without other balancing mechanisms) often create division within the organization. The group receiving the incentive views the departments that affect its performance as slow and nonresponsive. Rather than encourage cooperation between departments, bonuses can increase finger pointing.

It is often effective to adjust the reward or incentive. One car dealer found customers visited his sales lot at night to avoid obnoxious salespeople. The incentive (commission) encouraged salespeople to try to sell customers larger cars than they wanted—to maximize their bonus. After recognizing the problem, the dealer gave salespeople a fixed bonus for every car sold (based on average bonuses paid in the last year). Now rather than pressure customers, salespeople try to match a family's budget to the best car in that range. Sales increased dramatically.

Reward programs become part of the woodwork of a company in a very short period of time. They very quickly cease to motivate. For a while you saw many businesses with a picture of the employee-of-the-month hanging in the lobby or waiting area. Now you see very few. Why? One system was structured to recognize individual performance, so the most talented individual kept winning it. The rest of the workforce remained unmoved. In the other approach the award rotated between employees to keep it fair. The employees knew the award was not linked to performance and ignored it.

Incentives can suffer a similar fate. Money doesn't motivate for very long. A few months after a raise, people see themselves as being worth the higher income. At this point, the increase no longer motivates.

SUGGESTIONS

Rewards work best when they are fresh. They have a short life span. Use them to help start a new behavior. One company wanted to reduce lost-time accidents. They considered offering a company-provided lunch to reward employees for each accident-free month. Safe working is a good practice and should be encouraged. I suggested, however, that over time the employees might forget the relationship between the reward and the initial cause. They would come to expect the monthly lunch as part of an unspoken work agreement. If in the future, the company removed the lunch, the employees would react negatively. I recommended they promise employees a lunch for the first few months there were no lost-time accidents. After a few months, the practice of working safely should be a normal part of their job, rather than something to be continually rewarded. The lunch idea would then be available as an option to reward another new behavior the company wanted to encourage.

A correct reward or incentive, implemented poorly, is not effective. Both Seven-Eleven and a national department store employ professional shoppers to test and reward employee service behavior. A manager from the department store told me that when employees behave as trained they receive a nice letter and a $20 gift certificate many weeks later. For employees, the connection between behavior and reward fades after several weeks. When Seven-Eleven employees behave correctly, they can instantly receive $100 if they are shopped by a "phantom shopper." Employees know immediately what behavior is being rewarded. Which method would motivate you?

Rewards must be selective and infrequent to retain their value within the organization. If a reward is too widespread, it ceases to motivate. Use rewards to motivate *above and beyond the call of duty* behavior rather than normal job behavior.

Incentives are difficult to administer and powerfully drive behavior (sometimes in the wrong direction). As a general rule, proceed cautiously and consider the behavioral impact in all areas, not just the target job.

Implementation Issues

If you have new positions and departments, sit down with your colleagues and for each new position in the department ask yourself: "What will drive behavior in this environment?" It is an important and vital question. Try to consider the department and what it will be like. Then look at each job function and determine what would encourage appropriate behavior from those involved. Use the Reinforcing Structure™ as a guide.

The majority of managers, however, find themselves in an existing department with established behavior patterns. Some of these patterns are quite positive, while others may be less positive. In this situation, it is difficult to take the time to analyze all the key behaviors. Rather than abandon the exercise, try the following:

- As they come up, examine less-than-positive behaviors or problem situations. If you find employees are not behaving in a manner consistent with your objectives, ask the question: "What are we doing to encourage this less-than-helpful behavior?" The problem behavior is usually encouraged by some existing job structure.

- View every recurring problem as an opportunity to find out whether the organization is unknowingly encouraging the behavior. It often is. Be sure to build in some component of the Reinforcing Structure™ to reinforce the new activity. If you don't install an encouraging mechanism, the behavior will eventually go back to normal.

10

Explaining Improvement Simply

The Linear Progress Model™

STAGE 2 COMPANIES HAVE EXPANDED THEIR VISION to define the activities that lead to continued success. SMG's research found three core improvement dimensions within these organizations. The Linear Progress Model™ describes the three dimensions and their required activities.

The model is simple, visual and intuitive. It has been used effectively to help employees think differently about their work activities.

Barriers to Understanding

Employee reactions vary when you are discussing improvement. A few feel it is unrealistic to expect increased productivity; others are confused by the language; others are interested in seeing things stay the same.

Some employees hear "improvement," but see a drive for *more* work. They see signs of another productivity exercise. We have found the key to productivity is *not* working harder, as previously discussed *(Chp. 3)*. Working harder often means cutting corners, which increases variability and reduces productivity. We tell employees that productivity improves when you get rid of inconsistencies. The organization then avoids the frenzy that comes from cutting corners. The information contained in the Linear Progress Model™ and the Six-Step Process Improvement Method *(Chp. 10, 11)* makes employees comfortable with improvement.

Some are confused by the language of improvement. They correctly ask: "If improvement means that everything should be simple, why are the words so complicated?" Trainees learn fashionable buzzwords and intricate concepts. Theories sound fine in the training room, but employees find them impractical and difficult to implement. We believe employees and managers need simple explanations, simple tools, and structure changes to ensure everyone does their part.

Some managers can also be resistant to change. They have come up through the ranks and want things to stay the same. This type of manager is in love with control. They think through problems, then tell employees what to do. We believe managers should be motivated to facilitate change rather than hinder it. When managers' job structures are changed to encourage and include employees in decision-making, two things occur: organizations benefit when employees are involved; and most managers learn to appreciate employee participation.

Before employees can participate effectively, they must see the connection between vision and activities. The Linear Progress Model™ describes the three improvement dimensions: Operational, Customer and Human.

Each dimension has three milestones: a beginning, a middle, and an end. Organizational progress in shown in linear steps, starting from the left (or beginning), moving to an intermediate step (middle), and finishing on the right (end). A definition of each milestone is given for each improvement dimension, then the activities that allow an organization to progress from milestone to milestone are described.

Operational Dimension

The Operational Dimension involves giving people the freedom and knowledge to improve their activities. The intent is to provide the understanding or knowledge employees require, while allowing them to participate in the management of their processes. The Operational Dimension is concerned with doing things correctly so that delays and errors don't affect productivity and quality. It involves improving processes.

Processes? What is a process? A process is a series of steps that accomplish something. For example, a department uses a process or series of steps to handle customer returns or complaints. If products or services are delivered, there's usually a process at the center. Processes are the building blocks of business.

	Beginning	Middle	End
Operational Dimension	Correcting Defects	Consistent Processes	Productivity/ Quality By Process Design

The Operational Dimension describes operational improvement. When an organization begins to work on operational improvement, it starts by catching and correcting defects or errors in key processes. It has not yet learned to identify and resolve the root causes of these problems.

After working on reducing variability and streamlining major processes, the organization arrives at the middle of the dimension. It has achieved a consistency within its processes so that they can be counted on to deliver the outcome the customer requires.

After expanding its understanding of its processes and their limitations, the organization reaches the end of the dimension. The company now understands that quality, productivity and reliability are achieved through process design. What does that mean? It means the organization understands what it is capable of doing.

When a well-designed process is introduced, it immediately works well and meets customer requirements. In successful process design, there is a built-in understanding of what can realistically be expected. The organization continually takes steps to improve, but doesn't overpromise to customers because it understands what its processes can achieve. By promising more than processes can deliver, organizations can disappoint customers.

	Beginning	Req'd Activity	Middle
Operational Dimension	Correcting Defects	**Process Improvement & Consistency**	Consistent Processes

This diagram describes the activities required to move from one milestone to the next. For an organization to progress from catching or correcting defects to consistent processes, it must work on process improvement and consistency.

This means identifying key processes, streamlining them and building in consistency. Real operational improvement means reducing the number of required process steps and improving the consistency of those that remain. During the evaluation, most organizations find not every step is required.

During a client project that reduced four divisions to two, a problem with some technical software threatened to cause a month's delay. I was curious, so I asked to see someone use the software in question. I watched a technician painstakingly enter the week's information. The program was dreadful. Everything had to be entered many times and the divisional project would make it worse.

I asked who would be using the information. The technician thought for a moment and said: "I don't know." He had never seen any other department actually use the information. I inquired how long the technician had entered this weekly summary. The answer was seven years.

I suggested an experiment. He could stop entering the information and see if anyone noticed. During the next project meeting, I recommended no changes be made to the software until we were convinced the software served some purpose. During the next few months, no one noticed the missing information.

A change made years before made this particular task obsolete. For seven years, an employee wasted two hours a week entering information that was never used. Unnecessary process steps are easy to spot (if you ask questions).

Inconsistency in a process is much harder to recognize. The goal is consistent performance. It requires each employee to do a consistent job every day, in fact, every minute of every day.

Most business processes contain many inconsistencies. Poor communication, errors, and assumptions erode productivity and eat up time. As a result, organizations require additional time and resources to complete scheduled activities, even though adequate resources are made available. Variability or inconsistencies steal output. The reduction of process variability is discussed in detail in the next chapter *(Chp. 11)*.

	Middle	*Req'd Activity*	*End*
Operational Dimension	Consistent Processes	**Process Capability & Cust. Needs**	Productivity/ Quality By Process Design

To move from consistent processes to assured performance through process design, organizations must understand process capability and customer needs. The lessons learned while improving process consistency should be applied to new products or services under development.

The organization must understand exactly what it is capable of, if it wants new processes to enjoy high initial performance. Those designing processes must look realistically at what can be done. This doesn't mean we are satisfied with the company's performance. We can always improve. However, when we really understand what we can deliver, we can set customer expectations properly and keep them satisfied.

The Operational Dimension is concerned with *How we do what we do*. It is concerned with consistency, reducing unneeded steps and knowing what can realistically be expected from a process. As an organization works on its processes in this manner, it will deliver a more consistent product or service to its customers. Relevant questions here are: "What are the key processes?" "Are improvements being made in these processes?" "Are processes designed with the company's capability in mind, or are they designed based on *assumptions* of what can be done?"

Customer Dimension

To progress along the Customer Dimension, an organization must ensure that it understands what its customers want. It must set reasonable customer expectations and be able to deliver on them. This creates customer satisfaction.

When army warfare was simpler, the artillery pieces were not aimed with sophisticated electronics. They were guided by a spotter, who sighted the target so the artillery gunner could send off a shell. The spotter watched where the shell landed and sent back instructions to improve the accuracy. When the spotter was sure the range and position were correct, he would say: *"Fire for effect."* The army's resources could now be used effectively against the target.

Improving along the Customer Dimension is similar. The resources of the company can only be used to maximum benefit when the organization understands the customer's situation. Collecting the right information about major customers is essential if the organization is to *"fire for effect."*

Satisfaction is important for both external and internal customers. An external customer is one who resides outside the organization and receives benefit from the company's actions. An internal customer resides within the organization and receives material, information or services from other company areas.

	Beginning	Middle	End
Customer Dimension	**Specification Satisfaction**	**Customer Satisfaction**	**Customer Collaboration**

To improve in the Customer Dimension, an organization starts at specification satisfaction. This means the company is concerned with meeting the specifications developed by its own management or technical group. At the midpoint of the dimension, the organization understands the customer is the key source of evaluation criteria. The company is now concerned with customer satisfaction. A Stage 2 organization's goal is a mutually dependent relationship with the customer, which the model describes as customer collaboration.

	Beginning	Req'd Activity	Middle
Customer Dimension	Specification Satisfaction	**Research, Education, Benchmarking**	Customer Satisfaction

To move from concern over satisfying internal specifications to focusing on customer satisfaction, an organization must research what *external* customers want and need. The organization communicates customer requirements to its employees; progress toward these goals is tracked and encouraged. Tasks are completed so that *internal* customers can use the output immediately, without additional setup. This is a way of making sure internal customers receive information, products, or services in a ready-to-use format.

During the first phase of customer improvement, an organization moves from an internal to an external definition of what is expected. Techniques to discover customer perceptions can include focus groups, surveys, or just talking with individual customers. This information should be communicated to the rest of the company in a balanced manner to guard against a sales person talking to a single customer and trying to change the entire company's product or service offerings. If the comments are representative of the entire customer group, then a change may be appropriate. If objective research methods are not used, the resulting suggestions may hinder the company's efforts.

Middle	Req'd Activity	End

Customer Dimension	Customer Satisfaction	Involve Customers Earlier	Customer Collaboration

This figure describes the second phase of improvement in the Customer Dimension. How do we move from customer satisfaction to customer collaboration? You simply involve customers earlier.

Successful car makers are starting to involve potential customers far earlier in the design process, before mock-ups are made. Using computer-generated images, they obtain consumer reaction about potential instrument locations. By involving customers earlier, you reduce costly design changes later in the development cycle. This holds true for products or services.

In the case of internal customers, earlier involvement minimizes potential resistance and brings a fresh source of ideas to the situation.

There is an excellent example of early involvement of customers that predates the improvement or quality programs of recent years. Immediately after the second world war, Canadian aircraft manufacturer de Havilland planned to build a utility bush plane to fill under-utilized production capacity.

They sought the advice of bush pilots before creating a prototype, while the drawings were still on the board. They asked the pilots for constructive criticism, and they got it. The pilots suggested many enhancements that made the plane more forgiving, flexible and serviceable. The resulting Beaver was a more useful and productive plane. The Beaver was entered in bids for US Army and US Air Force procurement contracts in 1951, and won both contracts against a field of planes from 13 other companies. The rugged de Havilland Beaver became the benchmark for bush planes and was called the "general's jeep" during the Korean war.

Why did de Havilland's Beaver win the competition? They researched the needs of the customer and built the plane around those requirements. The result was a strong and lasting relationship between the customer and the company. This example shows how early customer involvement can lead to a mutually dependent relationship.

Before designing a new service delivery or production process, managers should ensure the organization understands what is required. The best way is to involve customers earlier, before things are firmed up and the decisions made. Progress along the Customer Dimension is attainable when the company knows what customers want, communicates to customers only what it is capable of doing, and consistently delivers products or services.

In the Customer Dimension, you learn *Who we do it for;* you ensure that your organization channels its resources for greatest impact, based on continual customer research and contact; and you learn to *"fire for effect."*

Human Dimension

Progress along the Human Dimension is more difficult than the other two dimensions. Why? Organizations quickly develop patterns of behavior and methods of relating. These patterns can be difficult to transform because they change slowly. If an organization has many layers of management, it changes even more slowly.

The objective is to develop and use employees' abilities to increase organizational effectiveness. This is essentially the empowerment principle that has been widely written about and, in most cases, poorly implemented.

People are empowered only when managers empower them. Some managers are reluctant to allow employees to make decisions. As they mature, these managers realize there is uniformity in control but precious little leverage. Today's organizations must leverage their human capital to flourish and prosper. Successful organizations have more than just a few managers planning and thinking. Successful organizations use reinforcing mechanisms like the Reinforcing Structure™ to guide and encourage behavior.

The Human Dimension describes this transformation process.

	Beginning	Middle	End
Human Dimension	**Control**	**Involvement**	**Stakeholders**

In the beginning, the Human Dimension shows management concerned or preoccupied with control: controlling employees; controlling activities; convinced that control is the secret to performance. Control is required to a degree and is totally appropriate. A heart surgeon, for example, does not want an assistant to experiment with procedures in the middle of a bypass operation. Both the surgeon and the patient want everything consistent and well rehearsed.

On the other hand, if you're providing a service and the customer has unique requirements, you may need your employees' creativity to provide what the customer wants.

As the organization progresses, management realizes it really *doesn't* control people, but it can *involve* people in managing their activities. Management *can* control the context or structure in which people work *(Chp. 9)*. The *structure* can encourage employees to continue to perform needed activities.

The midpoint is involvement, where a substantial percentage of the staff participates in improving the company. How employees become involved varies. Some are comfortable making suggestions face to face with management; others prefer less direct methods.

The Human Dimension ends with employees feeling they have a personal stake in the business. They become stakeholders. I didn't say shareholders, for equity ownership may not equal personal commitment. If people feel the organization listens, they can make a positive contribution and see the results of their involvement; they are then more likely to participate.

	Beginning	Req'd Activity	Middle
Human Dimension	Control	Process Ownership & Accountability	Involvement

This figure illustrates that an organization can move from preoccupation with control to involvement of people, if employees are given ownership over the processes they are involved in. Ralph Stayer's article "How I learned to let my workers lead," describes an eight-year journey to move his thinking and his organization from a position where few people participated to having a workforce that was actively involved in managing their processes. After eight years of evolution, employees were responsible and made decisions on a day-to-day basis.

Identify key processes and give people ownership and responsibility for those processes. Communicate the goals, objectives and vision through a business case. Ensure processes support strategic objectives. Remove obstacles. Review the behavior required by the process and put in mechanisms to reinforce those activities.

	Middle	Req'd Activity	End
Human Dimension	Involvement	Reinforcement & Modeling Behavior	Stakeholders

After employees become involved, the next step is to broaden and deepen their involvement so they become stakeholders. The objective here is to move from a focus on one or two processes to a broader understanding among the majority of employees. To move from involvement to employees as stakeholders, an organization must reinforce or institutionalize improvement behavior within daily activities. Management must begin to model this new perspective and express it in their actions with employees.

Why is it important for management to model the appropriate behavior?

One company in the research group successfully doubled productivity within the previous year. No additional staff were hired, but the multinational facility produced much more. "You must be thrilled with your improvement program," I said. The manager hung his head and said: "Well, actually the improvement program is dead." I asked why. Apparently, during a management meeting, the general manager commented that he had no use for the improvement material. He already knew how to make a business decision. He said he wasn't a "dummy." Within one week, none of the senior managers wanted anything to do with the improvement program. Within three to four weeks, the supervisors and employees understood the program was dead. Employees realized the promises made concerning a more collaborative, involved environment were empty. Productivity was up but morale went down.

There are many positive examples where management actively models this approach and gives decision-making responsibility to those involved in key processes. In cases like these employees seize their new responsibility and rise to meet expectations.

I recall a Friday afternoon session with a client's employees. One idea showed much promise, and rather than finalize the details within management, I gathered the individuals involved and asked for their opinion. For an hour or two they kept asking: "Have you thought about this or that?" I kept replying: "No, we brought you an idea that sounds good, but none of the details are decided. That's why you're here. Apart from meeting some overall objectives, the details are your responsibility." After repeating this six or seven times, they started to believe us. We finished the Friday with a stimulating discussion of some of the possibilities.

I was in the client's training room on Monday morning. A number of the employees who participated in the Friday discussion came into the room and each said in effect: "I've been thinking about this all weekend. I've got some ideas that may really help us." Their ideas did help.

The *idea*, to re-configure the operation, helped their plant to achieve a record sales year with less staff than before: at the same time the order lead time was cut almost in half. The *idea* became the cornerstone of the operation and one of the reasons the plant is now the leading producer within its group of associate companies.

The *idea* became the employees'. They saw it through. They demonstrated their involvement and without being asked, they spent some time on a weekend thinking about ideas. Why did they do that? They felt a personal stake in the success of the business.

The Human Dimension is concerned with *How we work together.* The objective of the Human Dimension is to have every (to be realistic, almost every) employee understand where the business is going, why it's important to get there, and what activities will help to ensure its survival and success. Although most employees are involved in only one aspect of the company, they need to feel a part of the whole. You accomplish this by making them responsible for and involved in managing their processes. Their positive behavior continues when you change the Reinforcing Structure™ or their job structures.

Individuals have long memories and progress in the Human Dimension is a moving average that gives some weight to today's activities but also includes actions from the past. This explains why many people aren't thankful and appreciative when management changes its behavior and goes the extra mile. They are encouraged by any positive change, but they want to see it last. Don't be discouraged. Persevere.

Are there *we* and *they* attitudes within your organization? Are there groups that have an animosity or a poor relationship with other groups? This is often a result of an out-of-balance Reinforcing Structure™. Managers are probably being measured on departmental or personal objectives, as opposed to broad, organization-wide objectives.

Support *people,* not the status quo. Help them to expect change. It is futile to expect tomorrow's results from yesterday's activities. Show them that although activities will change, your support for your employees will not. It is not wise, however, to start a broad improvement effort immediately before a significant reduction in staffing. It is better to wait for a stable period.

It is also damaging to have all the managers except one support the effort. Make your expectations clear to that manager. Change the Reinforcing Structure™ to encourage supportive coaching behavior and be prepared to act if six months to a year go by without improvement.

Using The Model

The Linear Progress Model™, with its three improvement dimensions, graphically explains the key activities involved in moving an organization forward. It also gives employees a common vocabulary to discuss improvement ideas and methods. Please see the back of the book for contact information to order reproducible masters of each of the improvement dimensions.

Individual employees or groups can consider the position of their organization (or department) on each of the three dimensions. Ask each member on a team to indicate where he or she feels the organization is and then discuss the differences in perspective as a group. The discussion will be both lively and profitable. The model can be used as a benchmark of progress in the three improvement areas.

Summary

The Operation Dimension describes *How we do what we do*. It is concerned with quality and efficiency. Process consistency helps to ensure productivity. It is people managing processes.

The Customer Dimension focuses on *Who we do it for*. This dimension encourages the organization to focus on customers' needs. If we are doing the wrong things, there is no benefit in doing them efficiently. The right things are defined by the customer; involve customers early in the development of any process or project.

The Human Dimension illustrates the steps required in improving *How we work together*. It involves people in managing their areas, reinforces positive behavior, and produces managers who, over time, model the thinking.

Improvement means real people become involved in improving their own areas, producing many small improvements over time. Improvement becomes evident when you reduce variability or inconsistencies in key processes. Improvement catches on when we reduce interdepartmental barriers by changing the Reinforcing Structure™ to reinforce broader perspectives. Finally, improvement becomes fun when people believe they can make a difference.

11

Six-Step Process Improvement Method

From Cost Reduction to Process Management

STAGE 2 ORGANIZATIONS HAVE MOVED from cost reduction programs to process management. The Six-Step Process Improvement Method gives employees an uncomplicated tool to improve their activities.

You may ask: "Aren't there enough process management tools to choose from?" Yes, there are a number of workflow, flowcharting, and problem solving tools available. Many organizations teach them.

Unfortunately, employees (and managers) don't use the majority of tools that are currently taught. SMG's research indicates very few trainees actually use these tools. Let me explain how we discovered this.

While working with a client's management team, the operations people discovered a problem and asked for help. A meeting was called to find a quick solution to the problem. I looked forward to observing the group in action because of their extensive training. The company had invested heavily—a significant amount per team member. In fact, I had rarely seen a company invest so heavily in training, so I thought I would learn a thing or two at their team meeting.

I was disappointed. No one wrote anything down. They talked only generally about the problem. After 45 minutes, they were no closer to resolving the issue. I began to use SMG's Balloon Diagram (explained later in this chapter) to identify the causes of the problem. Without showing them the diagram, I asked a few questions and recorded the answers.

In 25 minutes, we defined the problem, identified the probable causes, and selected activities to prevent the problem from reoccurring.

The initial wandering discussion didn't reflect their training. I asked the group why they had not used any of the tools they had been taught. They told me the tools and models were too complex and time consuming. They considered them hard to understand, even after their training. They said the tools required a long time to setup and complete, and represented a poor use of their time. As a result, they had gone back to just discussing the problem.

Their discussion did not identify the problem's causes or the resolution. I finally showed them the diagram that I had used to guide the discussion and asked them if they could use such a tool. They said: "That's simple."

The organization had spent a tremendous amount of money to improve problem resolution and the trainees had abandoned the material. I wondered how many other companies were in the same situation?

SMG completed a research project to identify the tools and methods that are being taught and the factors that affect usage. The survey showed trainees rarely used the tools. The flow chart was the only tool used by a majority of trainees in at least 10 percent of their problem solving discussions, and this was the most popular tool. All other tools had much lower usage rates.

Respondents found the tools too complex. They thought the material was unrealistic, more suitable for technicians and experts than workers. They also commented that the tools took too long to complete. Because of the time required and the poor results, management support evaporated quickly.

Most managers change tasks every nine to 15 minutes. Therefore, a problem solving model that takes hours to set up will not be used. The requirement is for simple tools to lead participants to the causes.

Pitfalls

Process improvement skills drive improvement, but a number of problems reduce process management effectiveness.

Not knowing how the process works now. Don't make changes without really understanding how the process currently works.

Not knowing how the process should work. By taking time to define the outcome of the process, you cut resolution time dramatically.

No preventive activities are planned. Change job structures to ensure preventive measures occur.

Unnecessary steps are left in the process. You should be able to justify the existence of each process step.

People involved don't have the ability to judge the process. The organization should provide expert help and training.

We don't know what we cannot do. The organization has not determined what it is capable of doing, so unrealistic expectations create unrealistic schedules which cause more problems.

We don't involve all the participants before changes are made. The resistance is predictable and preventable.

Management already has the perfect answer. Don't ask for opinions unless you can incorporate their suggestions. Prepare a draft solution, communicate the objectives, then ask employees to help complete the plan.

There are arbitrary limits on what can be suggested. Political interests stop profitable discussion. Resolve the political issues first.

The team has too broad a mandate. You cannot fix an entire company at once. Break the issues down by process.

Employees don't believe in group problem solving. Use a simulation or training exercise to demonstrate that additional perspectives on an issue improve the analysis and the potential resolution.

Method Steps

Organizations need a simple approach for people to adopt as their own. Streamlined Management Group's method has six steps. Some may say complex problems require a more complex tool. We disagree. Our experience indicates that the listed steps represent a significant weapon to use against waste, inconsistency and confusion. A simple tool yields better results than an unused tool.

One: Define The Process/Problem

As a manager, you will find two types of improvement situations. The six-step method is effective for both. Either there are specific problems to be solved or there is a process that needs to be improved.

When defining a specific problem, consider the processes associated with it when working through the steps. When working to improve a specific process, take your time covering steps one, two, and three. Process issues resolve more easily after the process and outcomes are well defined.

Define the objectives for your efforts. Briefly record the result you would like to achieve. Appoint someone to lead or facilitate the effort. Many people can be involved, but one person should coordinate the activities and meetings. It is important to select someone who will follow through on his/her responsibilities. The quickest way to extinguish enthusiasm is to leave someone in charge who does not do what he/she promised.

I don't recommend creating a fancy format for the group to use when documenting the process. Have them create their own. You can review it to make sure it covers the essential points. This helps them learn the method and makes the material their own.

Two: Document The Process/Problem

There is no one way to do this. Describe the outcome of the process. Record the requirements. Use facts, not adjectives. Don't say something is complete without explaining precisely what complete is and how it can be observed.

Identify the customers affected by the problem or receiving the output from the process. What do they require (from their perspective)?

PROCESS MAP OR PROCESS BLOCKING

Describe, step-by-step, the targeted process or the process under the problem you are trying to solve. List the inputs to the process. I don't recommend a very complex and time-consuming flow charting exercise. It won't improve the effort and lowers the adoption rate. I like to use the term "process map," because a map doesn't need to show every pot hole and every telephone pole to be effective. It need only have enough information to guide the observer.

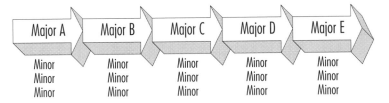

List the major process steps in a sequence of fewer than 10 points. List the minor activities within each major step. You will probably have anywhere from three to five minor steps for each major step.

Now use this map with your process improvement team to point out exactly where you will be focusing your efforts.

Three: Measure Current Performance

Measure the current performance of the problem or process. If you are working on a problem, record what you know about it. How often does it occur? Is there a pattern to its appearance? Does it accompany some other event or person? If you are working on a specific process, describe how it performs. You can measure performance in a number of different ways.

TIME

You can look at time measures: cycle time (the time required to complete one cycle of the process from start to finish); processing time (the cumulative time people or machines are acting on the information or material to transform it into the outcome); or delivery time (the time from first contact to receipt of the information or product).

ACTIVITIES

The number of activities can be reduced from the current total. The number of people involved or the distance traveled during the course of the activities can be measured and reduced.

PRODUCTIVITY

Productivity is the ratio of output compared to the required inputs. Your measurement will be more useful if it uses comparable terms or units of measure *(Chp. 9)*.

If you can document the current and revised performance for a process you are improving, you will find management support is much easier to obtain.

There are tremendous benefits to understanding the problem or the process. This is the result of the first three steps. They involve understanding exactly what is required from the process, who is involved, a full description, and a snapshot of its current performance.

Most organizations skip the first three steps and start at problem solving, but until a group identifies and documents the process and defines what is required, it often lacks the understanding needed to solve problems quickly and effectively.

Four: Understand Causes

The fourth step involves understanding "Why?" The group isolates one aspect of the process where there is a problem and uses SMG's Balloon Diagram to identify the root causes of the problem.

This tool is easy to use and particularly effective in identifying root causes. No mental gymnastics or abstract concepts are required.

The SMG Balloon Diagram meets all the key criteria required for a tool to be *used*. Most importantly, a group can complete a diagram in approximately 20 minutes, once they've practiced it a few times.

SMG BALLOON DIAGRAM INSTRUCTIONS

How to lead a problem solving discussion using a balloon diagram:

1. Define the problem. A narrow, well-defined problem is the objective. It takes a few minutes to discuss. Don't move on until the problem is clear to everyone.

2. Make sure everyone in the group understands the problem. Go to your process map from step two and point out exactly where in the process this problem occurs. This saves time and confusion.

3. Write the problem statement (a few words that summarize your problem) in the bottom circle on the diagram. *Artistically challenged individuals like myself should write the problem statement first, then draw the circle around it. I always draw the circle too small otherwise.*

4. Start by saying: **"What directly causes. . ?"** Then read the problem statement. Use the same three words every time. The group members will then see that there is really nothing difficult about the diagram and will be more likely to try it themselves.

5. As the group suggests direct causes for the problem, write each in its own balloon. Then draw an arrow from the cause to the problem statement below.

6. To encourage more suggestions, ask: **"What *else* directly causes . . ?"** Then read the problem statement again. Write down any additional causes in balloons.

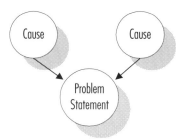

7. When it looks like you have all the direct causes ask: **"Are we done?"** If the answer is *no*, then continue. If the answer is *yes*, then go on to the next level.

Point to one of the cause balloons and start over again with: **"What directly causes. . ?"** Then read the cause statement. Continue to list the causes for each direct cause.

Normally you can go one or two levels. Here you either find issues you can discuss and fix, or you find questions that require investigation. The activity will then be to research the questions and find out the facts.

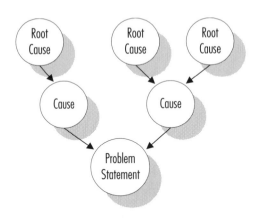

TROUBLESHOOTING AN SMG BALLOON DIAGRAM

Occasionally a group member will suggest something that isn't really a cause that contributes to the problem, but is something that occurs as a result of the problem. This is an *effect,* rather than a *cause.* To ensure that only causes (and not effects) are shown on the diagram, follow this simple method:

- Start at a balloon furthest out on one of the diagram's branches.

- As you read down toward the main problem statement balloon at the bottom of the diagram, you should be able to say: "This (referring to the outlying cause balloon) causes this (the next lower cause balloon), causes this (the next lower cause balloon) . . . " and so on until you reach the main problem statement.

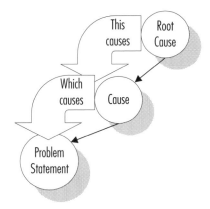

- If during your stepping down through the causes, you find one that doesn't cause the next lower balloon, you have probably found an effect (or a result of the problem rather than a cause). Remove or replace it with a cause.

Five: Develop Activities

After you've listed the cause balloons, the group can suggest activities that will either solve a root cause (highest level cause balloon) or gather information you need to fully understand a high level cause balloon. Draw these suggested activities in *activity boxes*. Activity boxes have three Ws: **W**ho (will be responsible for seeing the activity through to completion); **W**hat (in exact terms describe what must be done and how it should be done); and **W**hen (the deadline for the activity's completion).

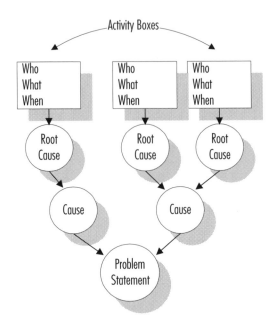

Six: Do & Evaluate

After recording the activity boxes, the group is free to complete each of the suggested activities. Ensure that each suggested action is under your control and that anyone who will be affected by an activity is informed beforehand. When more than one group member is completing the same activity, it is important to ensure consistent administration. Even a simple task can be completed by two individuals in two different ways, making the results impossible to combine. Define exactly *what* needs to be accomplished and *how* it should be accomplished.

After the activities are complete or under way, check the current performance against the pre-activity performance. If there is no difference, redefine the activities and try again. If you have made a difference, summarize on one page what the group did and what the result was. Communicate this to employees and to management. This will help encourage management support for future efforts.

Comments

The key to a successful process improvement effort is to introduce the six-step approach, then let the group experiment under your guidance. Your organization must fit the six-step method to its activities. See the back of the book for contact numbers to purchase reproducible masters your organization can use.

Have fun. Buy pizza for the group to celebrate the first problem solved. Make process management an enjoyable way of encouraging people to do their best and eliminate common frustrations. It will work, if employees understand the three dimensions of improvement *(Chp. 10)*, if they are allowed to practice the six-step method, if management encourages improvement activities via the Reinforcing Structure™, and if you make it fun. You won't be able to stop it. The key is to reinforce the behavior when it happens so it is more likely to happen again.

12 | Service Improvement
Ensuring Successful Customer Transactions

HERE ARE SOME PRACTICAL IDEAS FOR IMPROVING SERVICE DELIVERY. While a more in-depth look will be provided in SMG's next book, we thought it was important to go over the basics. Service employees are the people customers see first, but they frequently receive little or no training on how customers think and why they act the way they do.

We have all had disappointing service experiences, as well as experiences that renewed our faith in free enterprise. Large organizations don't have a monopoly on poor service, but due to their size and resources, they should know better. We have also seen outstanding examples of public service situations that would put the majority of for-profit businesses to shame.

Structure for Success

In general, structure and training are the keys to service success. If managers want to see specific behaviors from their employees, they must introduce job structures that encourage rather than discourage those behaviors. The training should help employees understand the way customers think.

The improvement method *(Chp. 4)* and the Reinforcing Structure™ *(Chp. 9)* equip you to construct service jobs that reinforce positive employee behavior. The Neat N' Tidy car rental example *(Chp. 4)* illustrates how a manager in a service environment can encourage needed activities to continue.

Managers should look at the organization as a whole and determine what behavior is required from each major part. When developing draft job structure changes for one area, it is helpful to examine the effect the resulting behavior will have on the rest of the organization. A small change may be all that stands between poor and outstanding service.

Example

One client complained that his sales staff were deeply involved during the sales process, but after the contract was signed, they disappeared from the scene. The information accumulated during the sales process, which was needed to meet customer expectations, was not being transferred to the rest of the organization. This caused errors, wasted time, and dissatisfied customers. Profitability also suffered.

Our client wondered what was wrong with the sales staff. He wanted them to *own* the customer's installation to ensure customer satisfaction and future referrals for the company. He thought if the salespeople were responsible, they would take the time and make the effort to ensure customers were properly cared for.

I asked how the sales staff were rewarded for their efforts (in other words what elements of the Reinforcing Structure™ was he using to motivate behavior). His company's compensation plan was designed to minimize any potential delay in paying commission. Under the plan, when salespeople closed a deal, they received their commissions within the month.

This policy was introduced by the owner who in his years as a commission salesman found it difficult to wait up to 90 days for his commission (triggered by the customer's payment). The sales compensation plan in his company was intended to encourage sales staff to close sales earlier. The owner thought the plan would increase sales and reduce staff turnover because salespeople would realize the plan was constructed to smooth out their personal cash flow.

He was *trying* to motivate his employees. However, he needed a broader (than just sales) perspective to correct the situation.

The compensation plan had some unintended effects. Because the commission was paid up front, salespeople had no reason (in their minds) to spend time with a customer after they signed. Their time was better spent finding new customers.

The lack of sales involvement caused several problems. The customer had to repeat everything that was communicated during the sales cycle to the installation personnel. As a result, the information was covered quickly, causing errors or assumptions to be made. The operations department worked under a disadvantage. Delays and errors meant service personnel had to make more trips than necessary.

I suggested a change to the plan: hold back a portion of the commission until the installation was complete and a satisfaction survey completed with the customer. This would give sales staff a reason to continue their involvement. It would ensure the rest of the organization had the information needed to guide activities. The result would be reduced installation time and increased profitability.

He made the change and sales behavior improved. In the following year, the company reported record sales, due in part to the continued involvement of its salespeople.

Customer Thinking

You only have to be involved in service delivery for a short time to realize it's different than most other functions. What makes service delivery so challenging? Customers, of course. They're all unique and some days it seems that each of them evaluates your service differently.

Leverage

Why is it important to understand how customers think? Leverage. For years, studies have shown that a satisfied customer will tell approximately seven others about your business. A dissatisfied customer will tell approximately 21 others about your company's mistake. A dissatisfied customer can hurt your business far more than a satisfied customer will help it. Is it fair? Of course not, but that's human nature. I guess people like to complain.

If you understand how customers think, however, your organization's ability to satisfy customers and build customer referrals will increase.

SOAR to the Top

One of the best summaries of service thinking comes from Dr. Mary H. Beaven & Dr. Dennis J. Scotti, faculty members at Fairleigh Dickinson University in New Jersey. Their model describes four elements of customer thinking:

The elements in their SOAR model are:

S	**Service scripts**	(reliability, courtesy, credibility)
O	**Outlay**	(money, time, effort)
A	**Accommodation**	(flexibility, responsiveness, access)
R	**Representation**	(realistic, clear, competence)

I have added tangibility to the Beaven and Scotti model.

| T | **Tangibility** | (easily seen, lasting benefits) |

The resulting model has five components, each emphasizing a different aspect of customer thinking. Following the Beaven and Scotti SOAR acronym, the adapted model could be called "SOAR to the Top." Let's define each element and discuss practical applications.

Service Scripts

Customers come to your business with a set of expectations (called a service *script*) already firmly fixed in their minds. Their expectations may be realistic or completely unrealistic. They also keep the majority of their expectations *private*.

When we provide a service, we hear customers' bare requirements. They tell us what they think we need to know and assume we will meet the balance of their expectations. During and at the conclusion of the service, customers evaluate the *perceived* service against their expectation set. Beaven and Scotti suggest customers may imprint on the first transaction they experience in a service category. They evaluate all similar service transactions against the benchmark of their first.

Service scripts are composed of:

• previous similar experiences;

• what customers imagine the service will be like;

• what they need the service to provide.

To simply communicate the concept of a service script (or expectation set) it is helpful to picture customers as icebergs, with a few spoken requirements above the water level and a great mass of expectations hidden below the surface.

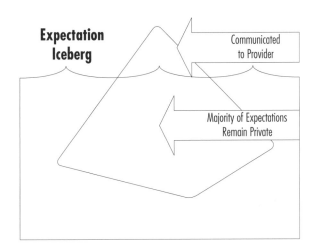

Expectation Iceberg

Communicated to Provider

Majority of Expectations Remain Private

As a result, you as the service provider must ask questions. Since the service script or expectation set is made up of at least three different facets, it is to your advantage to ask questions to draw out those expectations. Customers evaluate your service on their expectation set; not on your actions. It is their *perceptions* of your service delivery that matter.

- To draw out information concerning previous similar experiences, your customer service staff could ask customers: "Have you purchased anything like this before?"

- To understand what they imagine the service will be like, the question could be: "When you think about a successful transaction (purchase, installation, consultation), what kinds of issues are the most important to you?"

- To more fully determine customer requirements from the service, ask: "What other specific needs is this service going to provide for you?" or "After I read back your list of requirements, could you add any I may have missed?"

Record the answers from your questions. It will help paint a more complete picture of the criteria that customers will use to evaluate your service.

Asking questions takes time and is more appropriate for longer service transactions and less applicable for a business like a pizza outlet. The principle remains valid though. A pizza shop manager would not take time to ask each customer a series of questions, but should understand the expectation set for typical customers.

Reliability, courtesy and credibility are important considerations in meeting customer expectations. Another word for credibility is trustworthiness. A service continues to meet customer expectations by presenting a consistent, courteous face to each customer, every time. This requires that both the service delivery mechanisms and the underlying process are studied and refined to remove variability. The Visibility Map presented later in this chapter is a good tool to help you accomplish this.

Outlay

Outlay represents the money, time, and effort a customer must expend to produce a satisfactory outcome. Outlay describes the customer's estimate of the finances that must be committed, the time that must be spent, and the relative effort required to obtain the benefit.

Hidden charges cause dissatisfaction because they disrupt the customer's picture of the financial outlay required to secure the product or service. Hidden charges also damage trust between vendor and customer.

Time is frequently one of the casualties of the service revolution. Rather than tell the customer how long something will really take, organizations exaggerate (previously called lying), smile and mention a time frame they think the customer can live with. They don't want to lose the sale. When things don't turn out well and the customer is less than happy, the business will probably still get paid, but the customer will tell 21 other people how poor the service was.

The goal is to set realistic expectations in the customer's mind, then work like crazy to meet them. If you can't meet the time frame expectation, tell the customer up front and then emphasize other aspects of your service to keep your customer from going somewhere else. Work through the Six-Step Process Improvement Method *(Chp. 11)* to improve your delivery performance.

When there is a difference between the customer's perception of the effort the service should require and how difficult or frustrating the service experience actually is, customers become dissatisfied. One example occurs when customers phone in for information and are left on hold for what seems like hours.

Another example occurs at understaffed returns counters where impolite employees ask for two pieces of identification and dole out preprinted forms that customers must fill out. It takes a significant investment of time to return a product that only costs a few dollars and is purchased in a few moments. Customers frequently decide it is not worth the effort required to return the product or lodge a complaint.

Accommodation

The ability to balance consistency and flexibility frequently separates exemplary service from acceptable service. Flexibility in service delivery allows for customer differences, while still maintaining the essentials of the core service.

Since customers bring their expectations with them when they arrive at your business, it is not surprising that the identical service results in varying degrees of satisfaction for different people. Good restaurants understand the same food and service may not make everyone happy. Some customers expect special attention and test the limits of the delivery process. The story of a business person traveling with his son illustrates the principle of accommodation.

A man took his son on a combined business/family trip. They went to a restaurant for an evening meal and to discuss the next day's activities. The young man requested a hot dog and fries from the children's menu while the businessman asked for a salad and an entree. The salad and the hot dog arrived at the same time. After seeing and smelling the large hot dog, the man called the server over and said: "Could I change my order? My son's hot dog and fries look so good, I would like to cancel my entree and have the same. I'll understand if you charge me more than the children's menu price. Is that all right?" "I'm not sure" came the reply. "I'll have to check with the manager." After checking, the answer was unexpected and firm: "No sir. No adults are allowed to order from the children's menu. It's our policy." Despite his protests, there was no room for movement.

He quickly made two decisions. One, he would order another selection to salvage the evening with his son. Two, he decided neither he nor any of his staff would ever darken the establishment's doors again. There was no valid reason for denying the request. Perhaps the manager couldn't figure out how to enter a onetime price change for a meal into the computer system. Policies in a service environment need to be flexible.

Computer salespeople tell me first-time purchasers can be frustrating to deal with. No matter how diligently salespeople advise customers, they have difficulty understanding and meeting all their expectations. Accommodation for a computer retailer may mean setting up extra training classes for first-time users.

Accommodation is a balancing act. A service must develop consistency to minimize costs and to ensure quality and quick delivery. It must also allow employees flexibility to fill the gap between an individual customer's expectation set and the delivered service. Accommodation becomes the oil between the customer and your organization's machinery. It minimizes friction and keeps things running smoothly.

Representation

Representation describes the *accuracy* of the communication between your company and your customers. This includes advertising, brochures, press releases, internet content, and most importantly—personal communication by your staff. Customers' satisfaction largely depends on the *match* between your communication about your service and their actual experience of your service.

Customer satisfaction occurs when you meet or exceed the customer expectations. By overpromising you can make it virtually impossible to satisfy customers. It is better to slightly under-promise and then do a little more than expected to ensure you surpass customers' expectations.

I talked with the owner of a vacation resort. It was a prime location and the facility had been in his family for years. When a recession reduced attendance, an advertising blitz was organized. It brought in many new customers, including our family. The brochure promised waterfront suite lodging as well as an abundance of activities and above-average food. We found a beautiful main building with terrific food. We also found our suite was less than we imagined. Water-stained, paneled walls, worn outdated carpet and a moldy shower didn't match the impression given in the brochure. We changed to a slightly better room and ended up having a good vacation.

In my discussion with the owner, he candidly told me about the previous year. He had hired marketing consultants who promised to dramatically increase his resort's bookings. The consultants created new brochures that trumpeted the resort's features in glowing (and unrealistic) terms. This was the brochure that sold me on the resort.

The consultants' secret formula for increasing bookings was to instruct those answering the phones to say yes to anything if it meant getting a booking. It worked. Bookings increased, but so did the number of people left unsatisfied by the difference between what they were told and what they experienced. Repeat business dropped off significantly.

I encouraged him to try to set realistic expectations. The result would be repeat business, lowered advertising costs, and increased profits. I suggested some examples of more realistic descriptions for future advertising. The next spring, the resort employed my suggestions and their radio ads described a more realistic picture of the facility. But, it was apparently too little, too late, as a few months later I learned the resort had changed ownership.

All communication about your products and services must guide customers to a realistic view of your company's abilities and offerings.

Tangibility

Tangibility expresses how strongly the customer perceives the benefits of the service transaction. Purchasing a new automobile is quite tangible when compared with purchasing a new insurance policy. One transaction results in a bright and shiny car in the driveway, while the other results in a promise of assistance, which is much less visible.

Tangibility not only allows the customer to perceive the benefit of the service easily; it also clearly communicates the value of the service and how durable the benefit is.

Customers calculate value by comparing their perception of the benefits of the service with the outlay required to obtain it. Durability describes the length of time the actual service or the memory of the service exists.

When providing a service, you must make sure customers appreciate exactly what was done for them so they can include that information in their assessment of the transaction. The more the customer understands, the better the provider's ability to charge for the service. For short service transactions, you can list the activities on the order form or display them (nicely framed) in the entrance to your business.

For longer service transactions, like insurance, years go by without any personal contact. By paying a personal visit to customers to review their needs every few years, you help make the service more tangible.

For intangible services like consulting, it is important to remind customers of the complete list of benefits received directly or indirectly from the interaction. When the service is intangible, it is helpful to ensure that any tangible items (like reports) accurately represent your image and continue to remind clients of the benefits.

One travel agent had a creative way of increasing the durability of her service. At one time, the agent had provided a card and a bottle of champagne for couples on the first night of the cruise. This gesture was appreciated, but the champagne was usually consumed that night. As new experiences and memories accumulated during their cruise, however, the couple frequently forgot about the first night's gift. The travel agent decided to change tactics.

Rather than provide a short duration benefit, she purchased some good quality photo albums (with the title "Our Cruise" and her agency's name prominently printed on the front cover) and gave them to each couple. Now couples had a place to store the collected memories from their trip, and for at least the next year, the agency received free advertising. They showed friends and acquaintances the beautiful album. The duration of the gift went from hours to a year.

Now that you understand how customers think, you should evaluate your processes to identify customer issues. The Visibility Map will help.

Visibility Map

A Visibility Map is a specialized version of a process map *(Chp. 11)*. The difference is a line above the map. All process steps that are visible to the customer are brought above the visibility line.

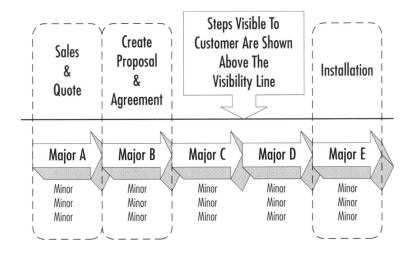

This shows a simple service example where the sales department identifies the potential customer and prepares a rough quote. Once there is sufficient interest, inside sales staff prepare a formal proposal, which becomes the basis for the agreement if the customer signs. The completion of the service is the installation or delivery component. This method of describing the steps can accommodate virtually any service delivery process.

The Visibility Map shows that there are two sides to the service process: the internal steps and those steps experienced by the customer. Internal steps should be reviewed to eliminate waste and minimize variability.

COORDINATION OF CUSTOMER INFORMATION

Care should be taken to carry all relevant customer information between the internal steps. This coordination of customer information is sometimes quite poorly done. Often the software systems used by service organizations are designed to collect and store all types of financial data, while there are very few receptacles for customer-specific information.

If there is to be a satisfactory outcome for customers, more information than the billing address is required. You must have the ability to communicate customer-specific information concerning how the service should be delivered. Normally, this customer information fends for itself outside the formal information systems, subject to variability and distortion. It is ironic that the most important information the organization has to secure customer satisfaction is often left to be collected and transferred informally.

The other effect of not having formal means to store customer information is a lack of coordination between steps in the process. The information, so carefully explained to salespeople, is often not evident during the delivery phase of the service. There is no formal way to inform the action part of the organization what customers expect or have been told.

If your software system is to be changed in the near future, ensure there are places to enter and record key customer information, so everyone involved understands what customers expect from your organization.

COMMON SERVICE EVALUATION CRITERIA

To use the Visibility Map effectively, follow these steps:

- show complete list of process steps;
- identify customer-visible events;
- identify key customer issues for each transaction;
- evaluate how you deliver on each;
- create an action plan to correct or improve service delivery.

Those steps that are visible to customers should be reviewed using additional criteria. The SOAR to the Top elements of customer reasoning will help to orient your service activity evaluation. The selection of additional criteria will depend on the nature of the service provided. A number of criteria for evaluating service activities follow:

Stability   Is your service consistent? Does it continually deliver on the promises made to customers?

Flexibility   Are you able to handle special requests and bend the delivery system in a timely fashion to accommodate unique situations? Flexibility must be in balance with stability.

Ability Do staff possess the skills and knowledge required to deliver the service?

Convenience Is the format (waiting time, hours of operation) suited to the customers or to those delivering the service?

Friendliness Are those delivering the service pleasant, polite and attentive to customers?

Clarity Do you communicate clearly, in plain language? Do you keep the customer informed, while listening for cues and signals that may require accommodation?

Trustworthiness Clear communication is not enough. You must ensure the accuracy of the impressions left with customers and the integrity of those involved in your company.

Tangibility Visible items should correspond to the image of your service. Ensure the benefits are easily perceived by your customers and that both the benefits and the recollection of those benefits last as long as possible.

Summary

Job structures that encourage positive employee behavior are a crucial part of an outstanding service organization. An understanding of customers' unique perspectives and the ways they evaluate your service better equip you and your staff to review present activities. The practical Visibility Map can easily and quickly be used to visualize service delivery processes. You can then examine delivery gaps and identify appropriate actions.

THE IMPROVEMENT TOOLBOX

13 | Facilitating Improvement
Developing Your Ability

THE ABILITY TO HELP A GROUP RESOLVE AN ISSUE or move toward a goal is highly valued in a manager. It is also an essential skill critical to a Stage 2 organization's improvement effort. Contrary to popular thought, however, you don't require an outgoing personality or a technical background to be a good facilitator. In our experience, the best facilitators are often quieter than most. They have learned through experience to value others' contributions and ideas.

If you know a few basics and are willing to learn, you can easily facilitate a problem-solving discussion. What are the fundamentals?

A Learned Skill

For all but a few, facilitating a discussion is a learned skill. It is not a technique for dominating a group. It is not just the collection of ideas. It is the ability to direct a group, to use their knowledge and experience to identify what they can fix or what they must investigate. Take any opportunity to put yourself in a facilitating role; review the following points; you will improve with practice.

The Key to Success

A successful facilitating effort isn't about trying to develop a happy or enthusiastic group. Success in facilitating is measured by activities and changes in your workplace. Participation is not enough.

I once led two teams at the same time for a client. The same under-standing was given to both. The same simple, practical skills were taught. One group made significant changes. Long-standing issues were resolved, errors were reduced, and productivity increased. A member from this group commented: "This stuff you're teaching is amazing. You must be a genius."

I agreed the material was practical, easily adopted, and effective. I also pointed out the reason everyone was eager to come to the weekly meet-ings was not me, but rather the changes the group made in their activities. The members were *doing* things and enjoying it.

He didn't understand. I told him about the other team. No one wanted to come. Everyone was discouraged. The same facilitator was teaching exactly the same material. What was the difference? Group 2 discussed what could be done, and then one extroverted individual volunteered to complete the task and report back to the group. The three following weeks the individual volunteered. Each following week, he brought excuses, not results to the meetings. After three weeks no one wanted to waste their time coming. The difference was in the doing. Group 1 acted and had fun. Group 2 did nothing and wanted to stop.

The key to facilitating success is not in stimulating discussion. It lies in following up activities so there are concrete results for the next meeting. People enjoy accomplishment.

Complete Tasks

During the discussion, you can use a process map, a balloon diagram or some other tool *(Chp. 11)*. To keep meetings crisp and ensure members respect your efforts, you must unfailingly complete any tasks that are as-signed to you before the next meeting. You set the pace. If you demonstrate that the meeting is worth your effort, others will contribute as well.

Help Others Complete Their Tasks

Your job doesn't stop with your assigned tasks. As facilitator, you are responsible for the group's success. The best way to keep people interested is to do things. Your job is to badger, encourage, motivate and help others to complete the tasks assigned to them. You have to be organized enough to start checking up long before the next meeting. Put notes to yourself in your personal calendar to bother, pester, remind and assist your colleagues in completing their assignments. If someone is unable to respond, then find someone else to complete the task or delay the meeting until the task is done.

Running The Meeting

Here are the key points:

BE PREPARED

Think about where the group will be going. Spend a few minutes familiarizing yourself with the material or subject area.

DON'T DOMINATE

Guide the group by asking leading questions. This is not the time for stand-up comedy (although a sense of humor doesn't hurt). Most of the time, members of the group should be speaking and you should be listening.

USE QUESTIONS

There are two different kinds of questions with specific uses:

- An *open-ended* question cannot be answered with a yes or a no. This type of question is the facilitator's favorite because it encourages further discussion. Use it frequently. An example is: "That's an interesting point; could you explain it further or give an example?"

- A *closed-ended* question can be answered by a yes or a no. It is useful to bring closure to a discussion or to establish agreement among the participants. An example is: "Do you all agree that XYZ may be a cause of our problem?"

KEEP PEOPLE INVOLVED

Ask someone to summarize the group's discussion before going on. Don't just speak with a few individuals. Ask quieter ones for their opinion, based on their experience.

LISTEN

When you begin to talk the moment someone else finishes speaking, you communicate that you were not listening. Pause a few seconds before speaking. If the comment is not clear or on topic, ask "Could you tell me more, I don't think I understand your point fully." or "Does anyone else see it differently?" Don't laugh or gesture when listening to responses. Use neutral comments like "okay" or "uh-huh."

HANDLE PEOPLE

Encourage shy people to contribute by making eye contact, using their names and asking for an opinion. Use body language to discourage those who talk too much. Look away if answers go on and on. This action will communicate your desire to move along. Ask other members for their evaluation of the speaker's comments to encourage more concise or thoughtful responses. When someone wants to take the group in a different direction, say something like: "Interesting idea, but today we're here to discuss _____." If you have people who share infrequently but feel free to judge other member's contributions, wait for a break and suggest they contribute positive alternatives rather than critique other's comments. If they cannot modify their behavior, remove them from the group.

SUMMARIZE

At the end of the meeting, summarize the session for the group. List accomplishments since the last meeting, what you accomplished during the meeting, action items (with assigned person and due date), and when and where the next meeting is to be held.

CREATE MINUTES

Appoint a recorder to keep the meeting notes for you in legible handwriting. That way, you can concentrate on leading the discussion. Good minutes can make a successful group much easier. Rather than opt for great looking typed minutes, I prefer a brief handwritten summary of the meeting items. The minutes should include a list of attendees, what you accomplished, outstanding action items with the date due and the person responsible, and the time and date of the next meeting.

After the meeting, the entire group can go to the nearest photocopier and get copies of the minutes. Members now know who is responsible for what activities and receive the written meeting record long before they would receive a typed copy. This increases the chances of activities being completed before the next meeting, therefore encouraging a successful group.

Summary

Being a good facilitator is a learned skill. Your success is measured by actual changes or improvements in the workplace, so the key is relentless follow up on the planned activities. If you complete your tasks and help others to complete their assignments, you will have a successful group. Come prepared to direct the group's discussion and appoint someone to take handwritten minutes for you. Use open-ended questions to encourage discussion and closed-ended questions to bring closure. Listen and pause before responding to comments. Encourage or discourage participation in order to obtain opinions from all. Summarize the accomplishments and assignments and decide when you will meet again. Thank the group for their time and participation. Duplicate the minutes immediately and make sure everyone gets a copy.

Between the meetings, follow-up to help your members complete their activities and you will be surprised at the results.

14

Coaching
Suggestions for Developing People

STAGE 2 ORGANIZATIONS DEVELOP THEIR PEOPLE. In fact, the development of staff is a hallmark of Stage 2 operations. Here are some practical
suggestions to improve your efforts.

FROM PERSONAL EXPERIENCE

I have coached little league baseball for four seasons. The team pictures
sit on my desk. My son just turned 13 and since he was nine, I have been
one of his team's three coaches. As the boys grow older, their abilities and
attention spans develop. While not major leaguers, the games are often
close, exciting and a showcase of good baseball skills.

During the years, I have studied other teams coaches. While most are
good role models, a few have extremely short tempers and take the house
league games far too seriously. I have also noticed that the same few coaches
are always in contention at the end of the year.

For the first two years, I thought these coaches had an in with the
individuals deciding the teams and were able to choose the better players. I muttered: "How can we get a team like that?" Then it dawned on
me—they were good coaches and that explained their teams' successes.
The other coaches and I dedicated ourselves to becoming better coaches.
We went to clinics to learn specific skills.

Although we have no idea which players will be assigned to our team, our standing in the division has improved each year. Last year we made it to the division finals and lost to a terrific team with five great pitchers.

Good coaches learn about players' strengths and weaknesses, help them improve, play to their strengths, and stay off the field—letting them play the game. I have read books about coaching in a business setting, but none affected me the way actually coaching has. Experience is a better teacher.

Finding opportunities to practice your coaching is important. At my children's school, the grade seven and eight students can volunteer to coach the lower grades' intramural sports teams. My son and another student were selected to coach a team. Their team went through the regular games, the playoffs, and won the championship. What a terrific learning experience for both of them.

I encourage you to try to apply these suggestions with your employees. Here are some things I've learned.

MAKE A TEAM

Good coaches usually don't start with an empty bench, but make the best of the group of players they have. Managers also rarely get an opportunity to start from scratch, so their job is to work with the people they have. Start building them into a team. If there are a few really bad apples, build a case to get them removed from the team, but first give them a chance to change their behavior by using job structures *(Chp. 9)*.

EMPHASIZE THE BASICS

Good coaches emphasize the basics and practice them until their team can do them well. Training doesn't stop when the season starts. All team members have to know their roles in the various plays and perform their parts even when they don't feel like it. Everyone is expected to practice well. We set the standard early.

Managers must know the processes within their areas and ensure their people know them inside out. Expect good performance from your people. If you expect mediocre performance, you'll get it.

WATCH FOR CRITICISM

We don't let players criticize each other. Our job is to encourage one another. If a player is clearly being critical of a teammate, we take the boy aside and remind him that we are serious about keeping positive and are willing to have him sit on the bench for a while to demonstrate our resolve. It is the coaches'—not the players'—job to deal with poor performers.

We never criticize players aloud during a game. They know they have made a mistake, because we practice the skills and they know what is expected. We offer encouragement from the bench. If necessary, we criticize privately by pulling a player aside and talking with him/her. If we started to criticize publicly, the entire team would join in and the mutual respect between the players and between the coaches and players would evaporate.

ENCOURAGE CONSTANTLY

The ratio of encouragement to criticism should be at least five to one (not scientifically proven, but it's how I like to be treated). Criticism should be focused on the behavior rather than the person. Telling people they are idiots does not build mutual respect—telling them they are letting the group down by not completing tasks may be more effective.

TREAT EVERYONE EQUALLY

We don't have superstars on the team. We do have players who demonstrate desire and ability, and have earned the right to play a certain position more frequently. In our league, every player must be moved around during the game. The rule keeps win-at-all-cost coaches from stranding a less-talented child out in right field for the entire game. Within these constraints, we put players in positions where their skills match the requirements of the position and still allow the team to play adequately.

By staying clear of favorites and treating your employees equally, you will spare them from many intergroup problems. Find out where they perform best on the team and try to use them there.

TREAT EVERYONE DIFFERENTLY

Recognize everyone is not exactly the same. We all have different personalities and different ways of learning. Some learn by doing; some learn by talking; and some learn very slowly. Every player is unique.

A coach's job is to find a way to communicate and to learn to read each player. You can then uncover problems before they become larger issues. You can help your team work on their weaknesses, but play them to take advantage of their strengths.

It may sound contradictory to tell you to treat everyone equally while at the same time telling you to treat everyone differently. The two thoughts are in balance, always in tension, and never perfect. Coaching can always be improved. Over time you can learn not to have favorites, to develop methods that build the team's performance, and still deal with people as individuals.

ADMIT MISTAKES

Once I forgot to signal a play during a championship game. The mistake cost the team an out that we could ill afford. The team thought the player involved had missed my sign. When I got to the bench I admitted that I had neglected to call the play and told the player it was not his fault. I try to act in the same way I want them to act.

Employees do not expect perfection. They expect a manager to work hard to get things right. When a mistake occurs, the best practice is to admit it and move on. If you don't admit an error, you give your people a reason to try to bring you down off your high horse. If you model the correct behavior, your team members are more likely to admit their mistakes before something major happens. That makes your job easier as corrective action is more effective if you catch a situation early.

VALUE THEIR CONTRIBUTION

At the end of each season, we have a cook out. We give awards and tell parents how their son has improved during the year. By the end of the season, we have learned to value each player's contribution to the team.

The cofounders of Kingston Technology of Fountain Valley California gave their 500 employees a significant Christmas bonus in 1996, the year they sold controlling interest in the company. The bonuses, based on seniority and performance, were one to three times the employee's annual salary! The total sum devoted to employee bonuses was approximately $100 million. When asked by a reporter why they decided to give such a large amount away, owners John Tu and David Sun said it was the employees who helped to build the company into what it was. As a result, their decision to reward their employees was quite easy to make. They learned to value their employees' contribution.

Everyone brings some talent to the company. Work at finding it and then learn to appreciate each contribution.

LEAD THEM SOMEWHERE WORTH GOING

At the beginning of the season, we tell the boys: "We're here to learn, have fun, and play baseball." We make a big deal about exhibition games and special trips. We try to make them feel the time spent with us will be worth it. There is no guarantee we will make the playoffs, but the journey will be a positive and fun experience.

People want to be special. In the 1950s, a workplace test in one company isolated a group of factory workers to show the effect of working conditions on worker performance. Surprisingly, as the testers made working conditions more difficult, performance improved with each change. Testers expected output to be reduced. One of the test group of employees was asked by a regular worker what the experience was like. She told her friend that the test group members had been selected because they were special and were able to handle difficult work. The results showed performance improved in spite of the conditions, because the workers felt they were special and able to perform well.

People will raise their performance up to expected levels. They will respond to your trust in them. Ask yourself why it is worth your employees' time and commitment to follow you, then tell them.

A TEAM HAS FOUR CHARACTERISTICS:

- shared outcome (possibility of success or failure);
- shared experiences over time;
- common purpose;
- trust and respect.

Trust and respect are both functions of time. Neither can be generated instantaneously. They are also both reciprocal. They describe the quality of a relationship, the connection between individuals.

Here is an evaluation that we have used in client situations. You can use it to measure your coaching performance. If you complete the test at the end of every quarter, you will get a picture of your progress and can take corrective action.

Rate Your Coaching Effort:

Number of personal decisions made during previous week ____

Percentage that could have been made by subordinates ____%

The percentage should go down over time. You make a number of decisions during a typical week that could be made by your staff, if you trained them and provided guidance. There will always be decisions that you must make due to your position, but as your staff develops and better manages their responsibilities, you would be freed to concentrate on the decisions that are yours.

Number of repeat decisions brought by subordinates during the previous week ____

A repeat decision concerns an issue that you have already discussed with an employee who should be able to handle it on his/her own. If you are building people, they should be bringing fewer routine decisions to you. Employees should make their own decisions based on agreed upon principles and then inform you, if required.

Rate Your Activity Focus vs. Goal Focus ____ **(1 to 10)**

1 = Only describe recommended activities to subordinates; you tell and they do (one person thinking).

5 = Describe goals & objectives with employees & discuss suggested ways to achieve them (occasional thinking by others).

10 = Describe goals & objectives with employees & they achieve them, keeping you informed (many people thinking, innovating, involved).

You can do all the thinking for your area and use the people who work for you as human tools or you can leverage the abilities of your people by setting the objective or goal in their minds and letting them accomplish it. One approach requires compliant people and the other requires competent, trained people. One requires a manager who is completely consumed with running the area's activities. The other requires a manager who leaves the day-to-day running of the area in the capable hands of staff, while planning where to lead them. One situation allows little time for training people, while in the other, the manager has found the time and the entire department has risen to a new level.

The best employees should be told only what they are to accomplish, rather than how to go about it. They find working in an environment where they participate in decision making to be rewarding, stimulating and fun. If managers are to leverage the intelligence within their area, they should concentrate less on communicating activities and more on communicating goals and objectives. They will gain engaged, involved and esteemed employees and make significant progress.

This is the same principle that Stephen Covey covers thoroughly in the excellent book, *The 7 Habits of Highly Effective People*. His term for activity focus is *production* and his term for goal focus is *production capability*.

STRUCTURING TO ENCOURAGE COACHING

If you have managers working for you who are reluctant to include subordinates in their decisions, the following reinforcing mechanism may help.

When you conduct performance evaluations for the managers, mention your desire to see them involve their people in activity planning and other decisions. Give managers time to improve. Ask them to create one-page reports describing specific examples from their departments. The reports would record in some detail, decisions that were made *after* subordinates were consulted.

Agree that for the next six months, the managers should each record at least one such instance each month. These monthly records then become part of their next performance appraisal.

There is now an incentive for managers to act in a positive manner. The motivation will help them to practice a more open decision-making style. It will also give managers time to experience the positive benefits of including people before changes are made. Remind managers periodically. If, after six months, they have no examples, they should probably not be on your team.

LEADERSHIP

Two of my favorite thoughts concerning the requirements of leadership,

1.   R. E. Thompson's tests for leadership follow:

- Do we use or cultivate (train) people?
- Do we direct or develop people?
- Do we criticize or encourage people?
- Do other peoples' failures annoy us or challenge us?
- Do we shun the problem person or seek him out?

2.   Lord Bernard Law Montgomery, who served the British as field marshal during World War 2, listed seven requirements of a leader in war. A leader:

- should be able to sit back and avoid getting immersed in detail;
- must not be petty;
- must not be pompous;
- must be a good picker of men/women;
- should *trust* those under his/her command and *let them get on with their job without interference;*
- must have the power of clear decision;
- should inspire confidence.

15 | Research Foundation
Ensuring Relevant, Tested Advice

THREE MAJOR RESEARCH PROJECTS WERE CONDUCTED to develop and test the models and the improvement method explained in the Improvement Toolbox. The survey work was conducted with an original group of approximately 70 organizations which were pursuing their own improvement strategies with varying degrees of commitment and resources. A large number of interviews added depth to the analysis and confirmed the findings. The SMG Improvement Method was field-tested with a number of clients to ensure the strategy worked.

This chapter briefly summarizes the three projects. The first project looked at the readiness or suitability of the organization to undertake an improvement effort and how certain factors affected progress. The second project looked at process management training, the tools being taught, and the factors that affect actual employee usage of the material. The third survey looked at the various means organizations use to create a sustainable improvement focus and the relative effectiveness of those means.

Improvement Readiness

This research project was designed to identify factors that would facilitate or impede the implementation of an organization-wide improvement effort. Improvement programs are a significant organizational change so the study concentrated on the activities and issues that affect the implementation of a large-scale change.

The investigation was completed in two steps. First, a model was created that described the essential elements of improvement and allowed progress to be measured (providing a ruler or gauge). Then, a number of factors thought to affect the progress of change were identified and tested in survey form using the model.

1. A MODEL THAT ALLOWS MEASUREMENT

The Linear Progress Model™ was used in the survey as a measurement instrument. Due to the simplicity of the model, a number of organizations were using the Operational, Customer and Human dimensions of the Linear Progress Model™ to explain improvement to their employees. Organizations had managers indicate their perceptions of progress along the model's three dimensions as a diagnostic tool, and then compared those results to the responses from the rest of the management team.

2. FACTORS THAT AFFECT PROGRESS

A number of factors were selected and included in the questionnaire as close-ended questions. They were designed to group the survey respondents into two (or three) groups (e.g., organizations with a champion and those without). Each factor was evaluated by statistically testing the average progress for each group on the Operational, Customer and Human improvement dimensions. If a factor was found to lead to significantly greater progress in two or more dimensions, it was considered to be important. The factors are listed at the end of this summary.

Features

- 72 organizations from both the U.S.A. and Canada, all geographic regions

- Over 144 organization-years of improvement experience represented

- Over 74,000 employees involved in improvement represented

- All sectors represented: Service, Manufacturing, Commercial & Consumer Products, Telecommunications, Transportation and Utilities.

Sectors Represented

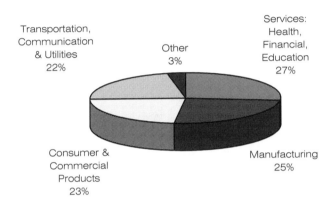

- Elapsed program time per organization ranged from 2 months to 5 years.

- Average years involved in program per sector:

Consumer and Commercial Products	1.7
Services	1.8
Manufacturing	2.1
Transportation, Telecom. & Utilities	2.3

RELATIONSHIP BETWEEN PROGRESS & ORGANIZATIONAL FACTORS

Based on the Linear Progress Model™ (using the key dimensions: Operational, Customer and Human), a number of factors were tested in the survey. The results by factor are summarized as follows:

The following factors were positively related to progress:

MANAGEMENT COMMITMENT

Greater management commitment meant greater progress in all key dimensions.

CHAMPION

There was higher progress recorded for organizations that had an internal champion. In addition, organizations with a champion from top management recorded higher progress than organizations with a champion from middle management.

TEAM PROBLEM SOLVING

Greater use of and effectiveness in team problem solving was strongly related to higher progress in all three key dimensions.

INTEGRATION

Organizations that had integrated their improvement program into normal operating and management activities recorded higher progress in all key dimensions.

LONG-TERM PERSPECTIVE

Organizations that had either long-term or a combination of long-term and short-term goals for their program recorded higher progress than organizations seeking only short-term goals.

TEAM PROBLEM OWNERSHIP

Organizations that let their teams select the problems they were to solve recorded higher progress (in the Customer dimension) than organizations where management either told the team(s) what to address or helped the team decide what to work on. Team ownership may be an important consideration.

These factors were negatively related to progress:

NUMBER OF MANAGEMENT LEVELS

Organizations that had three or less levels of management recorded higher progress than organizations with more levels. Implementing improvement within a deep organizational structure may be more difficult.

NUMBER OF EMPLOYEES

Organizations with 400 or less employees recorded higher progress than organizations with more employees. Perhaps breaking up into natural work teams may be a way for large organizations to obtain some of the benefits of being small.

VISIBLE PROGRAM START

Organizations that indicated they had a visible program start (kickoff meeting, etc.) recorded less progress than organizations that started quietly. There is a saying "Work underground as long as possible, for publicity triggers the corporate immune system." A visible program start may attract resistance.

The following factors were not related to progress:

EDUCATION APPROACH

There was no difference in progress between organizations that used a broad (organization-wide) education approach and organizations that used a narrow (departmental) approach to educating employees.

IMPROVEMENT OBJECTIVES

There was no difference in progress between organizations that had broad and general improvement objectives and those that had narrow and specific improvement objectives. The implication may be that programs should fit the organization's culture.

UNIONS

There was no difference in progress between organizations that had a union and those that did not.

CHANGE IN MANAGEMENT

Seventy percent of the organizations started improvement with existing management. There was no difference in progress between organizations that started due to new management and organizations that did not have a change in management.

AGE OF SENIOR SITE MANAGER

There was no difference in progress between organizations run by younger managers and organizations run by older managers.

MARKET GROWTH RATE

There was no difference in progress between companies in growing industry sectors and companies from sectors with no or declining growth. The assumption was that companies facing limited growth opportunities would be more likely to pursue internal improvements and therefore would be in the majority. The results did not support this assumption.

Problem Solving

The Problem Solving survey was designed to identify which tools are being taught, if and how often people are using them, and what issues keep people from using them. The hypothesis was that a tool increases the effectiveness of a problem solving discussion. One director said, "We left people alone at first assuming they knew how to solve problems. After a while, we found out they needed help."

The survey had a 20% response rate with 14 out of 69 organizations responding. A minority of the research group companies had conducted problem solving training.

Each responding organization was asked to give the one-page survey to up to five randomly selected individuals (problem solving trainees). The total number of actual surveys received was 56. Fifty-one were received in time to be included in the analysis.

Ten non-responding organizations from the study group indicated their environment did not lend itself to formalized problem solving methods. The reasons included: "Too little time available," "Things move too fast to write anything down," and "A formal approach would be too difficult for the individuals involved."

Highlights

- Half the respondents did the training within the last year.
- The majority (73%) of those who received problem solving training are now acting as facilitators.
- 80% of all respondents had some post-secondary education.
- There was no difference in education level between facilitators and non-facilitators.
- 71% considered their environment supportive of problem solving efforts.
- Respondents averaged one problem solving discussion every other work day (10/month).

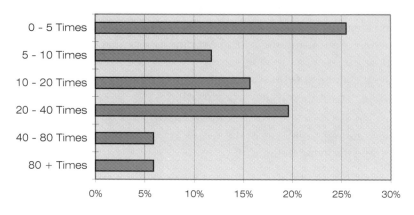

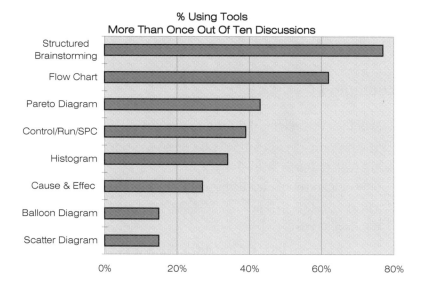

- The most commonly taught problem solving tools were the flow chart and the cause & effect (fishbone) diagram.
- Tools used most often: *flow chart* and *structured brainstorming*.

- Structured brainstorming is a non-written tool and often does not lead to the root cause(s) or provide confidence that the problem has been resolved. In simple terms, structured brainstorming involves talking about a problem. It is the *least* formal method and has the highest usage among respondents (Please see previous chart).
- The flow chart is the simplest formal tool and second in usage.

Issues Affecting Tool Usage

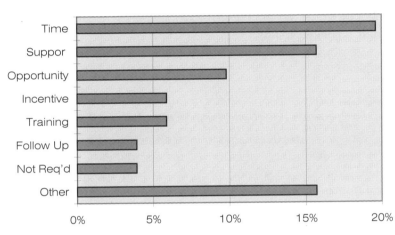

- Time constraints most limited the use of problem solving tools.
- Respondents cited various management-controlled issues as reasons for not using problem solving tools.

Conclusions

- *Time is important.* Individuals said time-related issues were the number one reason they were *not* using problem solving tools.
- A time-efficient, problem solving approach designed for *average* individuals is required.
- Problem solving doesn't just belong in the training room or board room. It must be simple and convenient and the training must be clear and concise.

Rate Of Organizational Change

The Rate Of Change Study was designed to identify the factors organizations perceive as critical to *continued* improvement progress. It was a one-year, time-series study with previously involved organizations responding to a survey similar to the original readiness survey. The survey had a 33% response rate with 22 of 67 original organizations responding. Organizations indicated the progress made during the year using SMG's Linear Progress Model™, which describes three key dimensions of improvement progress: the Operational, Customer and Human dimensions. The study highlights follow:

PROGRESS

Approximately one-third of the organizations experienced no progress in the Operational & Human improvement dimensions.

Nine percent of the organizations indicated they had experienced negative progress in the Operational (process) dimension and the Human dimension. The most common progress response for the Operational and Human dimensions was *zero*. Approximately one-third of the organizations experienced no progress in the Operational and Human improvement dimensions. If you combine the negative and the zero responses, 31% indicated no positive progress in Operational improvement and 36% indicated no positive progress in the Human (management) improvement dimension. One respondent commented "This stuff is hard."

SUPPORT THROUGH STRUCTURE

The survey looked at four different elements of a reinforcing structure: performance measures, evaluation criteria for employees, personnel rewards and incentives, and change in the organizational structure.

ORGANIZATIONAL STRUCTURE

In order to support the improvement effort, 41% changed the organizational structure but the majority (59%) left it alone. Teams dominated the changes in organizational structure, with 36% of respondents indicating they had put teams into the structure or had replaced individual managers with teams. Eighteen percent had entrenched quality reporting into the structure.

PERFORMANCE MEASURES

Forty-five percent of the organizations responded that they had changed performance measures to support their improvement effort. The amount of progress reported for the year appears greater for those organizations that changed performance measures (although not significantly—due to the small sample size). The majority of the performance measures introduced to support improvement involved customer satisfaction (36%) and time measures such as delivery time/cycle time (14%). Other performance measures that were introduced involved quality, safety, productivity, and cost issues.

EMPLOYEE EVALUATION CRITERIA

Forty-five percent of organizations changed individuals' evaluation criteria to support improvement. Seventy percent of the organizations that changed evaluation criteria changed them for all employee groups, whereas 30% changed them for selected employee groups. The most common criteria mentioned were quality and performance improvement. Also mentioned were performance against objectives, peer/subordinate feedback, and participation in improvement activities. Twenty-seven percent of the respondents indicated they would look at changing evaluation criteria in the future.

REWARDS & INCENTIVES

Forty-one percent changed personnel rewards and incentives to support their improvement effort; 59% did not. Of those organizations that adjusted rewards and incentives, 89% changed them for all employee groups and the remaining 11% selected specific employee groups to change. Just over half (53%) introduced or modified financial incentives and approximately one quarter (26%) introduced or modified rewards given to employees to reinforce improvement activities. A small number (9%) planned to look at this area in the future, while one organization didn't think rewards and incentives would be an issue for their employees.

CHAMPION

The presence of a champion affected progress. Eighty-six percent of the responding companies benefited from a champion, compared with only 9% that did not have one. Less than half (41%) of the champions came from top management. Exactly half (50%) came from middle management.

Half the organizations (50%) thought the champion's efforts had **decreased** over the past year. Twenty-three percent thought the effort from the champion **increased**, and 18% thought there had been **no change** in the last year.

For those organizations where the champion's efforts decreased, the most common reason given was that other business needs took priority. Other reasons included burnout and lack of management support. For organizations where the champion's efforts *increased*, the most common reasons given were strong management commitment and a perception that improvement was an essential part of operating strategy.

WHY?

Organizations were asked to give the primary reason for their progress or lack of progress during the last year. The most common reason for **poor** progress was a lack of management commitment. The next most popular reason was that other business issues took priority over improvement activities and pushed them aside. The most common reasons for **positive** improvement progress were *good management commitment* and *employee participation*.

WHAT ONE THING?

When asked what one thing would improve their improvement program, 41% of suggestions centered on improving management commitment, action or modeling behavior. Respondents also considered reeducating management, perhaps as a means of improving their commitment or behavior.

Organizations thought that changes in the reinforcing structure (performance measures, organizational structure, rewards & incentives, and evaluation criteria) and communication would help them improve their effort.

MANAGEMENT COMMITMENT

The most common reason for poor progress was a lack of management commitment.

Management Commitment

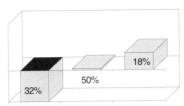

Decreased   No Change   Increased

Thirty two percent of the organizations thought that over the last year management commitment had decreased; only 18% thought management commitment to improvement had increased; and 50% saw no change whatsoever.

When asked why they thought management commitment levels had changed, respondents thought management took the focus off improvement and concentrated on other business issues.

Increased management commitment was thought to be due to management realization of the critical need to improve for both economic and business reasons.

Implications

The lack of progress for some of the responding organizations was surprising. A third of the organizations recorded no positive progress (in the Operational & Human dimensions); this is an indication of the way most organizations choose to apply these common-sense principles.

In most organizations, improvement activities are done *if there is time.* We believe that if improvement activities are woven into the fabric of the organization's business activities, improvement and regular activities will be inseparable. Improvement becomes an essential part of *how we do what we do.*

The questions relating to the four main elements of a reinforcing structure were meant to identify and measure the degree to which organizations institutionalized or normalized improvement behavior.

The four components of a reinforcing structure are:

- Organizational Structure;
- Performance Measures;
- Employee Evaluation Criteria;
- Rewards & Incentives.

In the graph, *mm. Change As Structural Components Added*, the average progress in millimeters (for each dimension) is shown for organizations that have not added any of the above components (in the none category). Also shown is the average progress for organizations that added any one or any two or any three or all four of the components.

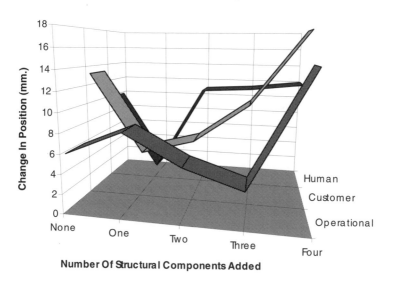

mm. Change As Structural Components Added

With only 22 organizations included, there are only four or five organizations in each category and we must be careful not to draw too much out of the data. However, it appears to show that as more structural changes are woven into the organization, improvement progress increases.

ENSURING POSITIVE PROGRESS

It is important for organizations to improve their *odds* or chances of achieving progress. Organizations must find ways to ensure activities continue. This is demonstrated by the survey results where progress responses became more consistent across organizations as structural elements were redesigned to encourage improvement activities. The reduction in progress variability was seen in a reduction in the range (or standard deviation) of progress responses among organizations (classed by the number of elements implemented).

Using the groupings from the *mm. Change* graph, you will observe that the results are described in the *Reduced Variability As More Structural Components Added* graph. As organizations add more of the four available components (of the Reinforcing Structure™), it appears there is a reduction in the variability of (or spread in) organizations' responses.

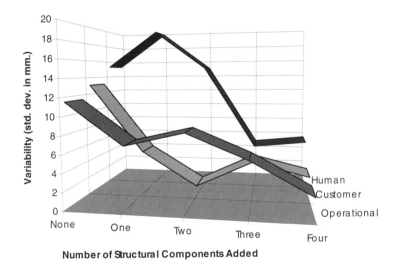

Reduced Variability As More Structural Components Added

This may mean that positive improvement behavior is reinforced, and more consistent progress achieved as organizations institutionalize or normalize improvement activities (into their performance measures, organizational structure, rewards & incentives and employee evaluation criteria).

As improvement behavior becomes more entrenched in normal activities, it becomes harder to separate improvement from essential business activities. This appears to be the key to preventing management from abandoning improvement for more pressing business issues.

MANAGEMENT COMMITMENT

Management commitment was reported to be the key reason for both achieving and not achieving progress. Eighty-two percent of the organizations thought management commitment stayed constant or declined, while only 18% saw it increase.

Why is this commitment so elusive? *Management commitment should be defined as everything except talk.* Commitment without concrete action is not commitment but merely marketing. The type of commitment a successful improvement program requires can be called Structural Commitment. In other words, visible and substantive changes are made in the working environment (Reinforcing Structure™) to support continual improvement.

CHAMPION

A champion does not guarantee improvement progress. Approximately 90% had a champion, but approximately one-third of the organizations did not record progress in two of the three main improvement dimensions.

MANAGEMENT LEVELS

Management levels or layers affect improvement progress. In the original readiness study, there was a difference in progress for organizations that had a champion from top management as compared with organizations with middle management champions. To change the structures within an organization, you need positional power and influence.

Recap

To see improvement activities continue, management must model positive behavior and change job structures to encourage continued participation and focus. Modeling requires a commitment that results in action.

It appears that making improvement an essential part of the work environment is the key. Management commitment is not an attitude. It is concrete action. Real commitment means management has changed structures to reinforce the new perspective and to ensure that other business issues don't crowd out improvement activities. Improvement then becomes the normal way of working.

References

Baetz, Mark C. and Paul W. Beamish. *Strategic Management.* 2nd ed., published in 1990 by Richard C. Irwin, Inc. Boston, MA 02116 (ISBN: 0-256-08340-1)

Beaven, Mary H. and Dennis J. Scotti. "Service-Oriented Thinking and its Implications for the Marketing Mix." *The Journal of Consumer Marketing,* (Vol. 7, No. 4, Fall 1990), pp.5-19

Covey, Stephen R. *The 7 Habits of Highly Effective People.* Fireside—Simon & Schuster Inc., New York, NY. 10020, 1990 (ISBN: 0-671-70863-5)

Montgomery, Lord Bernard Law. as quoted in *Spiritual Leadership* by J. Oswald Sanders. Revised Edition 1980, The Moody Bible Institute of Chicago, p.38

Stayer, Ralph. "How I Learned To Let My Workers Lead." *Harvard Business Review,* (November-December 1990), pp.66-83, Reprint #90610

Thompson, R. E. *World Vision,* December, 1996, p.4. (as quoted in *Spiritual Leadership* by J. Oswald Sanders. Revised Edition 1980, The Moody Bible Institute of Chicago, p.46)

Author Biography

Keith Miles is the founder and CEO of Streamlined Management Group Inc. (SMG). He is an author and management educator with over 15 years experience helping management and organizations transition to new activities and streamline processes. He received his bachelor's degree from the University of Western Ontario and his MBA from Wilfrid Laurier University, where he is a part-time instructor in Wilfrid Laurier's prestigious School of Business and Economics. He believes in having fun while working with groups and claims to have the best job in the world—meeting and helping people. He speaks at conferences and seminars across the country.

When not involved in his consulting business, Keith spends time with his wife and two children, enjoys sports and coaching his children's baseball teams, and participates in a local church.

Company Description

Streamlined Management Group Inc. is a management consulting firm with clients covering North America. SMG specializes in showing management and entire organizations how to move from Stage 1 to Stage 2 by teaching practical techniques to: link strategy with activities; shape employee behavior; and streamline key processes. SMG has a group of approximately 60 organizations participating in ongoing research from a range of industry sectors. Clients include: NCR, ITT, Rubbermaid, Equifax.

Ordering Information

Quantity discounts are available for bulk purchases.

Specialized versions of The Improvement Toolbox can be produced for volume situations.

Special excerpts can be created for specific needs.

Reproducible masters can be purchased for your organization.

Contact:

Business Development Manager

Streamlined Management Group Inc.

P.O. Box 31031, Guelph, Ontario N1H 8K1

Phone: (519) 822-3400   Fax: (519) 822-0333

Email: bus.devl@streamlined-group.com

Web: www.streamlined-group.com

1-888-843-4269

1-888-The I Box

For your convenience a fax form is printed on the next page.

Photocopy the form, fill in the blanks, and fax it to (519) 822-0333.

FAX ORDER FORM

Fax To: (519) 822-0333

Streamlined Management Group
P.O. Box 31031, Guelph, ON, N1H 8K1, Canada
Attention: Ordering Department

Price per copy $19.95 US + $5   Shipping and Handling
                 plus applicable taxes   (First Class Mail)
                 $24.95 Cdn. + $6   Shipping and Handling

Number of Copies _____ (volume discount rates will be applied)

Name (First, Init., Last) _____
Position/Title   _____
Company   _____

Send to Address: Home ____ or Business ____
Street Address: _____
Suite, Unit: _____
P.O. Box Number: _____
City: _____
State/Prov.:   ____
Zip/Post Code: _____-_____
Business Phone: (____) ____-_____ Ext. _____
Business Fax: (____) ____-_____
Person to reference on invoice: _____

Feedback / Comments: _____
                     _____
                     _____
                     _____
                     _____